IRELAND

BRENDAN LEHANE

FLINT RIVER

1989

ORIGINATED AND DEVELOPED BY
NEBOJSA BATO TOMASEVIC

DESIGNED BY
MIODRAG VARTABEDIJAN

IRELAND

TEXT BY
BRENDAN LEHANE

PHOTOGRAPHS BY
RICHARD NOWITZ

For *Flint River Edition*

A Motovun Group Book
© Flint River Press, Ltd, 1989
First Published in the United Kingdom in 1989
by Flint River Press Ltd,
26 Litchfield Street
London WC2H 9NJ

Distribuited by
Philip Wilson Publishers Ltd.
26 Litchfield Street
London WC2 H 9NJ

ISBN 1 871489 03 2

Text and captions:
Brendan Lehane

Design:
Miodrag Vartabedijan

Photographs:
Richard Nowitz

Editor:
Madge Phillips

Production:
John S. Clark

Project co-ordinator:
Una Tomašević

Colour separation:
Riproduzione Scanner, Florence

Printed and boud in Italy by
Sogema Marzari, Schio

CONTENTS

LAND AND PEOPLE
Around the Emerald Isle. The Lure of the Irish. Catholic and Protestant.
Cultural Imports. The Elusive Irishman. Gaelic English. Virtues and Vices.
The Chosen Race. Poverty and the Pub. Talkers and Singers.

ANCIENT IRELAND
Prehistoric Times, Myth and Legend. Pagan Kings and Celtic Saints. Monastic
Achievements. St Brendan the Navigator. The End of the Golden. Age.

NORSE, NORMAN AND ENGLISH INVADERS
The Arrival of the Longboats. The Anglo-Norman Take-over. Going Native.
Butlers and FitzGeralds. The Schism. Tudor Colonisation. Protestant Immigration.
William of Orange and the Battle of the Boyne.

THE AGE OF THE ASCENDANCY
Jonathan Swift and the Anglo-Irish Repression. Living like a Lord.
Dublin's Heyday. Great Anglo-Irishmen. The Stirrings of Independence.

FAMINE, RENAISSANCE, REBELLION
The Deadly Blight. Gaelic Decline and Celtic Revival. Yeats, Synge and the Abbey
Theatre. The GAA and Gaelic League. Militant Organisations. Easter 1916.

DIVISION AND INTEGRATION
Birth of the Irish Free State. De Valera and the Republic. The War and its
Aftermath. A Land Left Behind. North and South. Social Trends. Into Europe.

THE IRISH ABROAD

IMPORTANT DATES IN IRISH HISTORY.

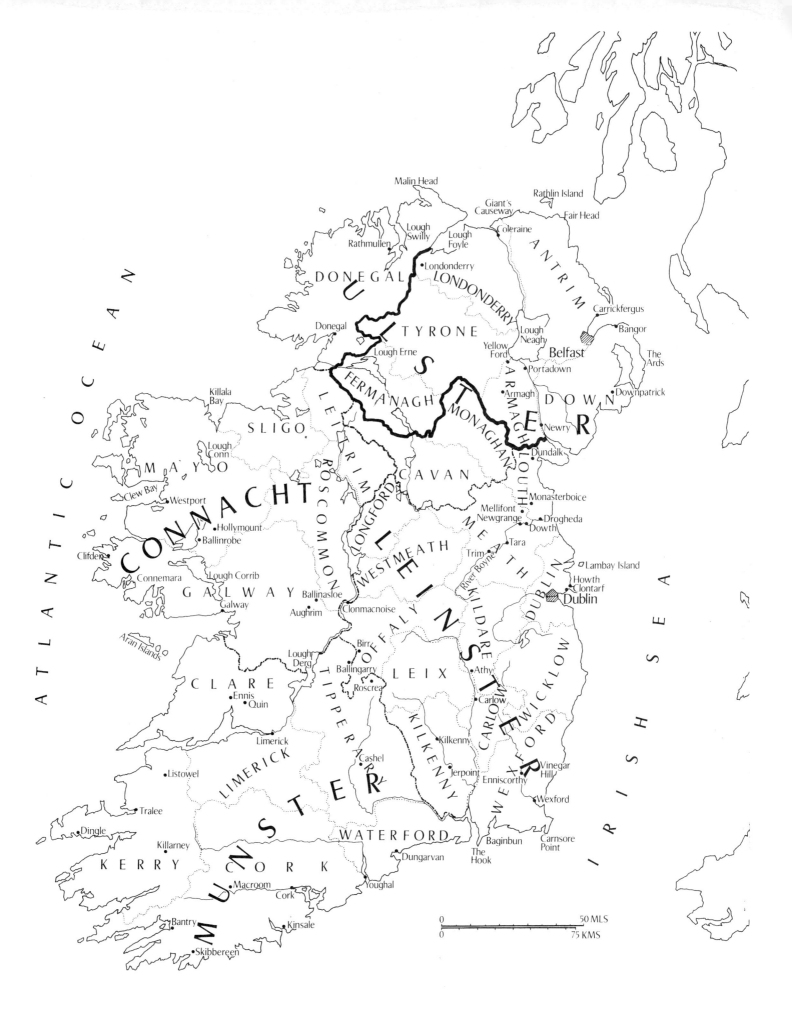

Malin Head

Giant's
Causeway

Rathlin Island

Fair Head

Lough Swilly

Lough Foyle

Coleraine

ANTRIM

Rathmullen

DONEGAL

U L S T E R

•Londonderry

LONDONDERRY

Carrickfergus

Donegal

•Donegal

TYRONE

Lough Neagh

Bangor

Lough Erne

Yellow Ford

Belfast

The Ards

FERMANAGH

Armagh
•Armagh

Portadown

D O W N

Downpatrick

Killala Bay

SLIGO

LEITRIM

MONAGHAN

Newry

ROSCOMMON

CAVAN

Dundalk

MAYO

CONNACHT

Lough Conn

Clew Bay

Westport

Hollymount

Ballinrobe

LONGFORD

Monasterboice

Mellifont
Newgrange

Drogheda
Dowth

Clifden

Connemara

Lough Corrib

GALWAY

WESTMEATH

M E A T H

Trim

Tara

River Boyne

Lambay Island

KILDARE

Howth
Clontarf

DUBLIN

Dublin

Galway

Ballinasloe

Aughrim

Clonmacnoise

Aran Islands

Lough Derg

Birr

OFFALY

Ballingarry

Roscrea

LEIX

Athy

Carlow

WICKLOW

CLARE

Ennis
•Quin

TIPPERARY

KILKENNY

CARLOW

WEXFORD

Vinegar Hill

Limerick

Cashel

Kilkenny

Enniscorthy

LIMERICK

Jerpoint

Wexford

Listowel

M U N S T E R

Tralee

WATERFORD

Baginbun

Carnsore Point

Dingle

Killarney

KERRY

C O R K

Dungarvan

The Hook

Macroom

Cork

Youghal

Bantry

Kinsale

Skibbereen

A T L A N T I C   O C E A N

I R I S H   S E A

0   50 MLS
0   75 KMS

Ireland:

Land and People

Around the Emerald Isle

Excepting Iceland, which is a long way off in the north Atlantic and scarcely belongs to the continent at all, the westernmost tip of Ireland is the westernmost tip of Europe. No European country is closer to America, and the Irish-American link is old and strong. But in the remote past, before America was known to exist, Ireland was at the end of the world. Beyond lay the boundless, unvarying ocean. Travellers — storm-driven merchants and fisherman — mentioned a land to the north, later charted by Norsemen and named Iceland. Westward was only sea. To the occupants of Europe's west coasts, though, it sometimes occurred that there was something more. Islands, cliffs, and sky-high mountains appeared to loom among the frequent sea-mists, or to stand out against the dazzling, apocalyptic sunsets. These incorporeal visions were given substance and names in men's minds. The Isles of the Blessed, Hybrasil, Lyonesse, Atlantis, and Tir nan Og — the country of eternal youth. With merit, or luck, the dead were conveyed to them to spend eternity in bliss. A few heroes visited them while they were alive. From these islands came gods and spirits to chasten or reward or inspire mortals. Up to quite modern times — some would say even now — the transient kingdoms of the Atlantic have exerted a powerful influence on the Irish, nourishing in them the dreams, imagination, the curlicued thought-processes and enchanter's vocabulary which characterise the Celt.

The eastern boundary of Ireland, a flatter, straighter, colder coastline, has a quite different prospect. It faces the grey waters of the Irish Sea, which separates Ireland from the mainland of Britain. This much larger country curves round the eastern outline of Ireland in what seems like the attempt of a governess to grasp an unruly child. The child looks to the Atlantic, to the sunset, to regions where the rules of reality are turned topsy-turvy. But she is held back. The interfering and pragmatic Anglo-Saxons will not quite let her go.

A line drawn from Dublin straight to the capital of any country in continental Europe, with the single exception of Portugal, passes through Britain. For much of her recorded history Ireland has shared a government and monarch with Britain. Even during her long periods of political independence, she has never been able to keep her eastern neighbour out of the reckoning. Geographical closeness has imposed on the two countries what family ties sometimes put on brothers and sisters who have little else in common: a need to take good and wary notice of each other.

The British connection has been even stronger than that. Her wealth has drawn innumerable Irish to enlist in her armies (providing half her best-known generals as well as numberless junior ranks), to build her railways and her roads, to minister to her

Roman Catholic congregations, and to supply a disproportionate number of colonial civil servants to the empire. It was Britain which unwillingly conjured out of Ireland generations of resolute insurgents, campaigners, freedom-fighters and terrorists, determined to break the political chains. In spite of all the blandishments of the make-believe west, Irish history can parade as much steely stubbornness as compliant charm. It is not entirely fanciful to represent these contrasting qualities as responses to the opposing pulls of east and west, the conflicting influences of England and the airy visions of the Atlantic.

Location, climate, rock, soil, fire and ice have all helped to shape and colour the land of Ireland and the curious and paradoxical character of her people. The soubriquet Emerald Isle comes from the greens of Ireland's grass and leaves, due in turn to the rain, which in the west at least occurs, according to statistical average, on every other day of the year, and in places tops 120 inches a year. It is a warm rain generally — the Irish call it soft — and seems sometimes no more than a misty spray which the breezes will evaporate within the hour. But it makes possible the rich growth of pasture on which much of Ireland's history and fortunes have been founded.

Though sharing latitudes with parts of Labrador and Alaska, Ireland enjoys the benefits brought by that oceanic central-heating system, the Gulf Stream, which pumps the tepid waters of the Caribbean to the western coasts of Europe. The consequence is that snow and heavy frost are scarcely known in most of the country, and that much of the west of Ireland supports vegetation more often found far to the south, in Spain and Portugal, or even the Alps. Various exotic orchids, the wild strawberry tree with its russet nuts and bell flowers, the bog violet which traps and consumes small insects, certain rare saxifrages and heathers, and to the astonishment of many visitors, mile upon wayside mile of crimson fuchsia and escallonia adorn the landscape.

The country thus formed by the force of the earth's movements and effects of climate is a small one: a bit bigger than Scotland, slightly smaller than Hungary; less than 300 miles north to south, and less than 200 miles east to west. Since its population is roughly equal to that of Istanbul, and a third of that lives in the five biggest cities, most of it is by European standards quite sparsely peopled. This is hard to believe on the spot because throughout most of the country, with the exception of the mountains, it is unusual to be out of sight of habitation. As one farmhouse disappears behind a hill, another comes into view. This is simply a quirk of history. A hundred years ago the great 19th-century estates were broken up and divided among their tenants. The average size of a farm became tiny by European standards, and in many areas remains so today.

Much of the centre of the country, stretching from county Clare on the west coast to Dublin on the east and from Carrick-on-Shannon in the north to Tipperary in the south, is a flat, but more often undulating, plain, with a few scattered outcrops of hills. To the north, south and west of this central plain are several ranges of mountains, mostly built upon cores of granite, though the escarpments of Antrim in the north-east are of basalt, a volcanic rock which on cooling forms naturally and picturesquely into six-sided pipes like hardened black honeycomb. The flattest areas of the central plain are formed from deposits of peat, or turf as it is known in Ireland, a soil formed over the last ten thousand years by the slow decomposition of moss and other plant matter. It covers about a tenth of the country's land area, and is known collectively and a little derogatorily as the Bog. Dug up and cut into pieces, it serves as a burning fuel in a country with hardly any coal seams, and its combustion in the grates of most Irish houses causes the sweet smoky aroma characteristic of towns and villages on winter evenings. For the Irish have not ignored this asset. A state-controlled company has charge of exploiting it, compacting the natural material into briquettes for ease of handling and marketing, or packing it for sale at home and abroad to gardeners seeking a fibrous, moisture-holding body for their soils.

To the traveller, though, the bog is chiefly remarkable as supporting mile upon mile of heather. In late summer the flowers come out, and in parts seem to turn the whole country purple, since many of the mountains are patched with peat as well. In bright sunshine there are streaks of silver among the purple, for the mountains are latticed with streams, and the plain cut by rivers and canals, while in parts of the midlands lakes seem to occupy more space than land. Kept constantly full by rain, they seldom have the strips of shore that surround lakes in other countries and mark the fluctuating levels of water.

The central plain consists of more than bog. From Meath, a county of rich farmland and estates north-west of Dublin, through Kildare and Leix to the Golden Vale of Tipperary is a loamy fertile crescent with soil as nutritious as any in Europe. Here are bred the same two animals which recur constantly in the most ancient tales of prehistoric Ireland: the cow and the horse. "This horse-riding, salmon-fishing, cattle-raising country," Yeats called it. Among the predominantly dairy farms of the west and beef farms of the east, but above all in county Kildare, are studs and stables which have sent forth some of the world's most successful racers. The horse might well have been a symbol of Ireland. It has been there for as long as man, providing him with speed and beauty, a fearless vehicle in battle and the hunt, and the perfect pretext for a bet and a drink. Its appeal — and there are not so many things of which this can be said in Ireland — goes beyond class and religion. The training establishment near the Curragh racecourse may boast glinting white gates, lawns trimmed with razor blades and the elegance of an 18th-century villa for the reception of Americans, Arabs and Japanese, but as likely as not the owner will spend his happiest hours at the bareback beach races of county Kerry, where indeed he may find his most promising future stock.

The actual official symbol of Ireland is, of course, the harp — played by wandering Gaelic singers up to the 18th century but scarcely seen now. The unofficial symbol is the shamrock, a plant whose leaves are divided in three, and which St Patrick supposedly used to explain the nature of the Trinity. Everybody wears the shamrock on St Patrick's Day. The curious thing, however, is that nobody seems sure what plant it should be. There are rival claims for the lesser yellow trefoil, wood-sorrel, white clover, black medick, hop-trefoil. The contrast between the plant's central role and indeterminate definition constitute an Irishism, a class of paradox to be met with again and again.

Having so much space, the Irish have tended not to knock down rural buildings which are no longer used. Thus another commonplace sight of the hinterland is the ruin. The farmer builds his new house — almost certainly a bungalow with an arch or two and the tang of the Costa Brava — well away from the old, which he leaves to the mercy of time and the weather. Grand mansions, abandoned or burned by accident or design, have become hulks of stone softened with ivy and evoking the ghosts of their heyday. The gravestones beside crumbling Protestant churches stand at drunken angles among briars and anthills. Castles, towers, monasteries, forts, cells and monumental graves from the earliest periods of man's occupation are to be seen all over the country, neither tended nor razed, simply permitted to stay on until the ground they occupy is needed for something else. Not the least spectacular class of ruin is the monastic round tower, which may be up to a hundred feet high, and was probably used for summoning the faithful 1200 years ago in the same way as the minarets it resembles.

Apart from hurling matches, horse races, and the manic rush of anglers from the cities as soon as the first mayfly is seen to rise from the central lakes, the attractions of the hinterland are relatively restrained and quiet. By and large, Ireland's scenic dramas are close to the sea, and a majority of them to the western rather than the eastern sea. True, the mountains of Wicklow are on the east, allowing the Dubliner to be swallowed up by rustic lanes, beside forested valleys and tumbling torrents, or on the bare hillsides with only lark and lapwing for company, less than an hour away from his city's centre. Fifty miles north of Dublin the mountains of Mourne roll down to the eastern sea, and north again those of Antrim, cut by their nine wooded, watery glens. But between these outcrops lie tamer lowlands, many of them edged by unbroken miles of white sand beach. But for sustained dramatic spectacle it is the west coast which leaves all the rest behind.

Till well into this century little attention was paid to this fact. Life in the west was hard. Sea and rocks claimed many of the fishermen who put out in the skin and wicker coracles that have been used in these parts for at least two thousand years. Over the centuries the land had been divided according to the Celtic system of equal inheritance into ever smaller portions, bounded by walls of the ubiquitous stones which made the land so unfruitful. Only a generation or so ago the signs of poverty abounded: children with hollow, staring eyes and matchstick legs, skeletal cattle tethered among the windblown scrub, one-storey cottages — cabins, some people still called the smoky Irish homes — with slumped roofs of mossy, mouse-eaten thatch and a turf-stack leaning against one wall. A few tourists came to Killarney and Connemara, but not enough to alleviate the penury and hunger. Then, suddenly, things were changing fast. The dreamy Irish gave scope to their practicality and created a tourist industry so effective that the English and other nationalities came to learn how it could be done. The west opened up. Young people who would otherwise have emigrated to England or America for work, as countless Irish had done for a hundred years and more, found employment in hotels, catering, or any of the ancillary activities tourist require. Shannon airport, opened in 1945 as a customs-free transit depot, became the gateway to the west for travellers from all over the world. They might head north to the precipitous cliffs of Donegal, to a corner of which the characteristic colour of the blazing sunsets has given the name Bloody Foreland; to the bosomy Ox Mountains of Sligo, on one of which a massive nipple of stones is said to be the grave of Maeve, ancient queen of Connaught; to the bare and moody moorland of Mayo, or the Twelve Pins of Connemara rising from a blue-green lakeland; to the Aran Islands, whose natives speak Gaelic and whose surface soil, every cubic inch of it, was humped here by humans in the form of seaweed and sand, or to the Burren, a curious lunar landscape of limestone slabs and inordinate interest, for in the fissures dividing these slabs grow orchids and other rare plants. (An English officer of the 17th century saw nothing to detain him among such features. The terrain, he wrote, yielded "neither water enough to drown a man, nor a tree to hang him, nor soil enough to bury." It was clearly beneath contempt.)

South of the airport the lure is no less. Across the broad estuary of the River Shannon lies the county of Kerry, its gnarled sandstone ranges pointing like bony fingers into the Atlantic. From one of them, some ancient documents seem to say, an Irish monk sailed into the ocean some fifteen hundred years ago and discovered America. The tip of another, the vertical rock of Skellig Michael, pummelled by wind and wave and often inaccessible, still carries the remains of the monastery that once provided a desolate home to a company of brave ascetics. Not many miles away the gentler contours of the Great Blasket Island support a numerous flock of sheep and a single-street ghost village. The last of its residents were removed in 1953 by order of a government that asserted life was too harsh and barbaric there, a curious claim given that in this century alone no less than three of the islanders — Maurice O'Sullivan, Peig Sayers and Tomas O Crohan — had written memoirs which will without doubt remain for ever in the canon of Irish classics.

Just inland from these rocky promontories is Killarney, with its picturesque placements of mountain, forest, river and lake making it one of Ireland's most beautiful

Irish (Iona and Kells): St Matthew, from Book of Kells. 760–820. 13 by 9½ in.
Trinity College, Dublin

*St Matthew, miniature from the Book of
Kells (760-820), one of the most lavishly
ornamented of all Celtic manuscripts,
named after the monastery of Kells
(county Meath), to which it was taken
from the monastery of Iona, where it was
written and illuminated.*

features, if not the jewel in the crown. Queen Victoria herself came, as did many of her distinguished subjects. Today it gets almost impossibly crowded and boasts American and German as well as Irish hotels. At least it acts like the jam-pot to the wasp and keeps adjacent areas relatively uncluttered. South of it, county Cork maintains the alternation of promontory and inlet until it rounds the corner to a coastline which though less sensational is far from dull. These are the fields and fences where the amiable characters of Somerville and Ross's novels hunted, drank and bantered their lives away; and further on, inland from the city of Cork, is Blarney Castle, whose lord in Tudor times resisted Queen Elizabeth's demands with all the charm and fair words at his disposal until the despairing sovereign burst out: "This is all Blarney; what he says he never means." Blarney has ever since been held to mean a facility with words unmatched by action, alleged to be characteristic of the Irish.

Further along this south coast the River Blackwater occupies a bosky valley, sometimes overlooked from the top of steep slopes by mansion or castle; and so likened by partisans to the Rhine. Gradually the coastal heights give way to long broad beaches (the Irish say strands) and gently curved hinterland. (It is seldom hard to find privacy on an Irish beach; overcrowding where it occurs is due not to want of space but to most people's passion for company.) Waterford's harbour cuts a broad swathe inland and at dawn and twilight rings with the sad calls of its numberless water-birds. There are beauties everywhere: dunes and marshes, abrupt islands, castle-capped headlands, distant views of the Wicklow peaks. But less drama. We have reached the east again, and while the east evokes a serene contentment, the west takes the breath away.

The Lure of the Irish

Settle a Spaniard or a Rumanian in Ireland and he, or at the least his children, become no longer Spanish or Rumanian but Irish. It was the despair of the medieval English that every wave of colonists they sent to anglicise Ireland became wholly Irish, even to the wearing of modish Irish whiskers and yellow cloaks and fighting the next incursion from the homeland. That process of assimilation still works. What causes it is open to argument. Is it nature's work or man's? Nature has made Ireland a rich tapestry of landscape, unlike any other; given it blown-out volcanoes akin to Scotland's, deep firths as inviting as Norway's, sands like Morocco's, light as pellucid as that of Greece, valleys of Tuscan loveliness, tides from the Antilles, salmon from Greenland, plants which are cousins of those in the Alps, swans from Iceland, sunsets like Turner's, and an extremely wet climate. Is it these ingredients of the Irishman's daily diet that work on all who come here and mould them into Irishness?

Or is it the things that man has made, the everyday experience of rural Ireland — for Irishness affects everything. Fields and farms are small, hedges thick, and lanes wind narrowly under the uncannily vast sky. Grandiose gateposts flank entrances to tracks that lead nowhere. Signposts specify distances in miles or kilometres and quite often, deflected by wind or leprechaun, or just possibly young humans, point in a wrong direction. Sheepdogs rush at car wheels. Villages boast inordinate numbers of pubs, the owners' names in bright bold uncial capitals above curtained windows, and, inside, the ceilings tarred with smoke. There are grottoes holding statues of the Blessed Virgin Mary, and for some there are sights of the Mother of God herself. At times of mass the neighbourhoods of churches are choked with cars.

Some would say that the essentially Irish agent that goes to work on the settler from abroad is not unconnected with these signs of piety, but that it is broader and older than they are: an aura of spirituality, magic even, which seems palpable in numberless places in Ireland. Some might claim it is a product of the country's history, different from all others in Europe in that the Romans never came, never occupied the land, never imposed their discipline, sense, symmetry, logic and straight roads. It could be strongly and plausibly argued that all these are ancillary influences, and that the force that works the change is the personality of the Irish people, with whom we shall become closely acquainted in these pages.

Rome's absence counted for much. Ireland reached the Middle Ages in a state other nations had cast off centuries before. True, she was Christian, devoutly and devotedly so. But her social organisation and institutions, her language, literature and entertainments, her laws and wars and feuds, even aspects of her Christianity, harked back to an era before both Christianity and Roman dominion in Britain. She was to remain, into quite recent times, a historical anomaly, out of step with the rest of the world, usually shuffling along a few paces behind Britain in matters of material progress, technical development and fashion. A distinguished Irish archaeologis, R.A.S. McAlister, has said that in Ireland the Stone Age survived into the 20th century. It would not have done so had the legions, whose commanders did consider the move from the facing island of Anglesey, sailed and disembarked.

Beyond a certain point speculation on the question is fruitless. One fact remains: the Irish are unlike anyone else, wholly their own people. Then again, they are wholly unlike one another, which makes generalising almost impossible. The Irish are beyond doubt a racial motley, with much Celtic blood, much Scotch (another branch of Celtic) and much from the veins of those who inhabited the country before the Celts arrived. But blood, as we have seen, signifies little. Till recent years it was reasonably assumed that people of Anglo-Saxon extraction would be more common in the east of Ireland, those of Celtic stock in the west, to which in the days of English settlement dispossessed natives were generally sent, and where the Gaelic language has survived most strongly to this day. The two races, as it happens, belong to different blood-groups. Thus, when a nationwide medical survey in the 1960s showed that the Anglo-Saxon blood group predominated in the far west, and not least among Gaelic speakers, there was surprise and embarrassment. It seems that 17th-century English soldiers were paid with parcels of western land in greater numbers than anyone had realised. Three centuries later, their descendants were wrongly taken to be the purest representatives of the ancient Celt.

So the blood of the Irish gives nothing away. The part of Ireland they come from may tell something. The born Dubliner, like cockneys and other big city products, is shrewd and quick. The Kerryman is allegedly a little slow. He is the man who is said to know anything he does know because he is too lazy to forget it; or when charged with some crime, refuses to plead on the ground that he has yet to hear the evidence. Certain citizens of Mayo inherit the qualities of avarice and cunning, while the Ulsterman is honest and industrious. There are plenty more such clichés, possessed of more truth or less, but never to be relied on.

Catholic and Protestant

The main badge in Ireland, the thing each Irishman wants to know of a newcomer before categorising him, is religion. Education, media, the characters of parents, wealth and class form the Irishman no less than they do other peoples. But in Ireland religion cuts through those distinctions and is the prime mark of identity. Not perhaps religion in the strictest sense. Every Irish God-fearer fears the same God, the Christian

God. (There may be 2000 Jews in the country; hardly more than a handful of other beliefs). Religion rather in the sense of culture: of the community one belongs to, the families among whom marriages occur, the pubs one frequents, the schools one's children attend, social events. Irish religion has some strong affinities with class divisions. Specific religious differences — habits of confession, belief in transubstantiation, acknowledgement of the leadership of Canterbury or Rome — are tied in with all of these. So too, as with everything, is the attitude to England. Without something of the religious geology of Ireland, knowledge will always stay on the surface.

Roman Catholicism was always the religion of the majority, and so it remains. The Republic is well over ninety per cent Catholic. In the six counties of Northern Ireland only a third are Catholic, but the overall national total is still almost three quarters. This is evidenced not only by questionnaire and survey; visible church attendance by young and old bears it out, and the lists of masses hanging outside churches in the big cities can be as complicated as railway timetables. Catholicism has strong links with nationalism, with a certain resentment of England, with the wish to revive the ancient Gaelic virtues, with the independence of the Republic and with the memory of those who fought and died for it. For many Irish it symbolises a spirit which existed before the English came and which survived everything the English could do to eradicate it. The symbolism may not be very appropriate, since the Church was often divided in its attitude to nationalism. While parish priests tended to identify themselves with aspirations to liberty and in many cases came out openly to fight for it, the hierarchy was generally far more circumspect. Time and again it condemned nationalist agitators, even the most heroic of them, and actually excommunicated several of them.

Conversely, many of the foremost campaigners for independence — indeed, up to this century the majority of them — were Protestant. But they were exceptions. By and large and predictably, the association between Protestants and Britain was stronger than that between Catholics and Britain. That association was complicated by the existence of two main Protestant groups in Ireland: the Anglican Church of Ireland on the one hand, and the Presbyterian Churches on the other. The total numbers of these two Protestant bodies are roughly equal, and together with Methodists and Baptists they account for about a fifth of the total population of the country.

Protestants are much more numerous in the North, where they make up two thirds of the population, than in the Republic, where they amount to no more than a twentieth. Presbyterians in the North are more numerous, by about four to three, than members of the Church of Ireland. These Presbyterians are descended from Scottish settlers of the 17th century, whose religion was based on the puritanical and uncompromising doctrines of John Calvin. For much of the period since their arrival the state recognised only the established Church of Ireland and laid heavy penalties on all who did not conform to it. Presbyterians suffered along with Catholics and other nonconformists. They had no reason at all to feel brotherly sentiments towards Anglicans, nor any love for the government at Westminster. However, if they disliked England they loathed Irish nationalism even more. Morally strict, disciplined, and hard-working, they looked on Catholics as feckless, lazy dreamers, duped by the superstitions and idolatry of the Church of Rome. Were they to be cast politically adrift from England in the same boat as the Catholics, everyone, they felt, would sink. When the time came, they resisted independence and preserved six of Ulster's nine counties as part of the United Kingdom. They also retained the rigour of their views. In terms of the geographical draw, they looked steadfastly away from the sirens of the western ocean and kept their feet firmly on the ground.

In all this their attitudes and actions were widely different from those of their fellow Protestants in the established Church of Ireland. This was for centuries the

17th-century woodcut illustrating the slaughter of Gaelic Irish Catholic rebels. According to the inscription, those "who drowned not were killed with poles and shot with muskets".

Church of the ruling class, the landlords, settlers of the 17th century and later who remained obstinately English in Irish eyes and obstinately Irish in English. Wealthy, powerful, remote, occupying grand houses, owning vast tracts of land, devoted to the horse and known collectively as the Ascendancy, these were the Anglo-Irish: "no petty people" said the poet Yeats, who claimed to belong to them; rather "one of the great stocks of Europe." Ireland's independence, won in 1921, removed their prestige, and most left for England. Those who stayed in the new state had no ruling to do: their loyalty was suspect and they would not have been welcome in most political parties, though some wanted to play a part in shaping the free Ireland. Many of them still had — still have — fine houses and horses, and land or investments enough to maintain them. But history has left most of them high and dry, eccentric and somewhat irrelevant ornaments.

Not that the rulers made up the whole Church of Ireland congregation. Behind the squire's family pew were ranged the merchants, agents, bailiffs, tradesmen and various professionals and their wives and families, who underpinned the glittering canopy of Ascendancy rule, determinedly distinct from the papist peasantry. They too fled in large numbers in the 1920s. Most of those who remain, if they resisted assimilation, live in Dublin, which in this respect is as untypical of Ireland as New York is of America. More widespread relics of Anglo-Irish days are their buildings: the redbrick Georgian streets and squares that once made Dublin the most charming city in these islands, the village churches which are so much older and mellower than Catholic churches (which were forbidden till the 19th century), and the elegant mansions and castles among the noble trees of their abandoned estates — or demesnes — which are still seen all over the country. Astonishingly, the Church of Ireland retains two cathedrals in Dublin, while the Catholics have none. Several proposals to surrender one of them have been scotched.

Cultural Imports

children by hund:
ting them into Riuers,
killed with poles &

G

Religion in Ireland, then, is almost synonymous with culture, though within each religious sect are wide cultural variations, brought about by differences of wealth, occupation, district. Where North and South are concerned, district can be paramount. It surprises many to know that a Northern Catholic may have more in common culturally with a Northern Protestant than with a Catholic from the South. Competition plays a part here, that careful scrutiny of the enemy which may sometimes lead to emulation of his virtues. But then boundary lines between groups have been smudged by the tide of modernism brought in by the last fifty years of television, tourism, and newspapers, by the European Community, and by a greater personal affluence which enables vast numbers of Irish to spend their holidays in England, America and elsewhere. The doubtiest western shepherd or fisherman will turn out to have visited cousins in England, America or both, and been visited by them. He may well have drunk Guinness in the bars of Chicago and the pubs of Shepherds Bush. He may for a while have held a job in the Philadelphia police.

The signs of imported cultures are everywhere. American styles pervade shops, eating places, clothes and clubs. All down the east coast of Ireland the television masts sway twenty or thirty feet above the houses they serve, catching programmes from Britain (many of these American), which seem less provincial than native products. The palpitating music which accompanies the meals, work and leisure of young Americans and English marks time for the young Irish too. They fleck their accents with mid-Atlantic effects, and their earnings here, as elsewhere, attract media, advertisers, promoters of rock, fashion designers, drug dealers. The high proportion (for Europe) of young Irish receiving advanced education, and growing familiarity with the world of silicon chips and computers make them still more cosmopolitan.

Somehow, though, these skeins of influence do not quite conceal the permanence beneath. Not even the self-conscious difference between generations does that. When a Catholic mother gets into a car, they say, she crosses herself (by way of an appeal to God) and, despising new-fangled gadgetry, refuses to fix her seat belt. Her daughter does the precise opposite: fixes her belt, but abstains from what she sees as voodoo. But the underlying Irishness comes through. The daughter doubts the existence of God, never her Catholicism. Like two in three of her generation, she will go to mass every Sunday.

The Elusive Irishman

Amid such disparities it may reasonably be asked whether an Irish character, a composite Irishness, may truly be said to exist. Is any useful denominator so common that it straddles these cultural chasms? Love of an idea of Ireland, certainly. Not so much as to stem a steady, two-hundred-year flow of emigrants from all communities to Britain or America — a flow which was only temporarily checked in the 1970s and has since recommenced. But enough to keep them, once arrived in their adopted countries, resolutely Irish in loyalty, friends, habits, and nostalgia. Yet that means loyal to their religious and cultural origins. The domestic divisions persist in London, Liverpool, Glasgow, Boston, Philadelphia; and the composite Irishman is as elusive as ever.

He does exist, though. He exists in literature, and you always seem to be meeting him in real life. He tends, it is true, to belong to the Catholic community, which once commanded the whole of the country and which, after all, still comprises the overwhelming majority in 26 of the 32 counties. But if he is partisan, his traits are nevertheless uniquely Irish. They are not found in English Catholics or Spanish Catholics. Not all his attributes are admirable, and there are those whose dislike of the preponderance of faults over virtues in the portrayal of their countrymen leads them to resent his reputation and even deny his existence. This, they say, is not a real character, but the stage Irishman, invented by the English out of bias and bigotry in order to justify their rule; the real Irishman has as much that is earnest, prosaic, calculating, ambitious and accomplished as the Anglo-Saxon, or any other racial representative. It is quite true, he does. But in an uncommon number of cases he manages to conceal it. He does this with a kind of character cosmetic which brings to the surface all that is agreeable and charming, and keeps below it all that is otherwise. It is well, therefore, to remember that the amiable, feckless, somewhat whimsical character described in Irish jokes, Irish novels, and stories of encounters between tourist and native, is merely one side of a character who, for instance, won his independence by a deadly and ruthless devotion to his cause, and whose ancestors were said to be able to kill by the cruelty of words. And to recall that the stage Irishman is not on the boards twenty-four hours a day. Out of sight, it is possible (though extremely unlikely) that he beats his wife and bullies his children.

Of course the Irish are logical. One plus an Irish one is two, and Irish night follows Irish day as surely as any other kind. Yet by some curious alchemy, and perhaps to the exclusion of other elements, the Irish take their logic a little further than others. Irish jokes show this in practice. They almost always seem to make a mockery of good sense, or one palpable truth is given priority over another. Two adversaries about to duel with pistols decide that the one of them who is short-sighted will stand ten feet nearer to make it fair. Such twists are known as Irish bulls. An inconsistency is concealed

1. *The limestone landscape of the Burren region in county Clare, south of Galway Bay, seems stark and bare: mile upon mile of broken stone pavement. It conceals wonders. Cracks between rock slabs nourish rare orchids, gentians, and other plants found nowhere else in the country. Miles of natural subterranean tunnels lie below, with cave systems beloved by speleologists. And the remains of stone age dolmens are scattered over the surface.*

2. *The shadowy outline of Knocknarea in Sligo. The protruberance on the surface (1978 feet high) is a huge cairn of loose stones about a hundred feet across, estimated to weigh about 40,000 tons. Thought to be a bronze age tomb, it is known as Maeve's Grave, Maeve being an ancient mythical queen of Connaught.*

4

3. On the north-east coast of Ireland the mountains of Antrim fall to a curious outcrop of patterned rock. This is volcanic basalt, which on cooling forms polygonal columns, mostly of five sides, but four, six and seven are found. Folklore prefers the account that it was constructed for the fabulous giant Finn McCool as a path to Scotland.

4. The dolmen, a huge stone cap resting on three other stones, is found all over Ireland. A form of megalithic burial chamber, dating from about 3,000 BC, originally it was probably covered with earth and stones, and the cremated remains of the body would lie among precious objects to be enjoyed in the life to come.

5

5. Few countries are more favoured with harbours than Ireland, whose northern, western and southern coastlines are pierced by long thin firths, fjords and estuaries. Except in the most fashionable resorts, there is seldom a shortage of space for anchoring sailing boats.

6. Promontories dip down to the sea and end in a tail of diminishing islands, too small and inaccessible for use. But Ireland is ringed too by large islands — Rathlin, seen here from the Antrim coast, Tory, Aran, Achill and so on — populated for centuries but in many cases now cleared because they did not warrant the vast cost of installing modern services.

7 and 8. In the 19th century, when geology was an infant science, many scholars were convinced that the honeycomb formations of the basalt rock which makes up the Giant's Causeway in country Antrim were man-made. Fingal's Cave and other similar formations off the west coast of Scotland suggested a basalt road had once linked the two countries. The two are indeed linked underwater, but the regular shapes are quite natural, formed by cooling basaltic lava.

9

9. *Clifden, a resort on the west coast of Galway, with the Twelve Bens of Connemara in the background. The church on the left is Protestant, that on its right, Catholic. Clifden is the setting for the annual Connemara Pony Show, held in August.*

10. *The sheer face of Benbulden in the Dartry Mountains of north Sligo. On its summit, Dermot, once the lieutenant of the giant Finn McCool, slew a huge wild boar, but was in turn killed by the poison of its bristles, ending a sequence that began when Dermot eloped with Finn's betrothed Grania. The poet Yeats is buried at Drumcliff, nearby.*

11. *The population of Irish donkeys has dropped drastically in recent years. A generation ago the donkey-cart was a universal means of rural conveyance for people, peat, market produce and so on, but the car has superseded it.*

10

11

12. Though it must be one of the oldest activities in the world, and dogs can be trained to it, nobody has ever perfected the art of rounding up sheep.

13. In the past, the sight of traditional cottages might have been enough to enable a lost traveller to locate himself; there were great regional variations of roof-shape, type of wheat or oats used, decorative 'dollies' along the ridge, and means of securing the thatch. Now uniform new cottages spring up everywhere for holiday homes.

14. *Boggy stretches in moorland and on mountain sides can make walking rather hazardous. In recent years the proliferation of forest parks all over the country, and National Trust properties in Northern Ireland, has meant an abundance of nature trails, tracks and maintained paths for the less adventurous.*

15. *One of Ireland's two remaining windmills, at Tacumshin in the country's south-east corner. Built in 1846 (and reconstructed in 1952), it is known as a tower-mill. The cap revolves in order to take best advantage of the wind.*

beneath what sounds quite reasonable. Sir Boyle Roche in the early 1800s debating a tax that would benefit future generations asked the Speaker of the Commons why so much trouble should be taken for posterity. "What has posterity ever done for us?" And on another occasion, "I don't know," says the modest Irishman, on a pheasant shoot, complimented for bringing down a bird; "I don't know; sure to God the fall would have killed it anyway!" Elsewhere a gloomy Irish poet opined: "It's only the hope of dying that keeps me alive."

Gaelic English

More often than not the sweetness of the reason is matched by that of language. The charm of the Irish use of the English language is in no small part due to the practices they brought with them from Gaelic, which was spoken by half the population only five or six generations ago. Some of these are basic. Irish lacks exact translations of the English "yes" and "no". Asked whether they will do or say something, the Irish tend to reply "I will" or "I will not". For similar reasons, "I have been to the shop" is rendered "I am after going to the shop". Irish verbs have a habitual tense, expressing continual action, as seen in Synge's description of certain dead bishops as "the like of the holy prophets do be straining the bars of paradise to lay eyes on the Lady Helen," ("the like of" for "like" is another Irishness). The listener is to understand that the exertions of these good men is no flash in the pan, but a habit. A practice which colours much Irish speech is that of invoking the aid or blessing of the deity or a relevant saint at every pretext. "By the Lord and all the holy angels," or "May God be with you" or "Mary, Mother of God" are parts of everyday speech, scarcely less automatic than the "honestly", "I mean", "frankly", "in fact" with which the English punctuate their speech. But more charming.

The master of this transposition from Gaelic to English was John Millington Synge, to whose plays the international fame of Dublin's Abbey Theatre at the beginning of the century was partly due. He recorded that as a young man he rented a room on the Aran island of Inishmore to increase his knowledge of Gaelic. The room happened to be above the kitchen, and a crack in the floor enabled him to hear everything the girls below were saying. He took down all he could, and in due course gave speeches inspired by this dialogue to his own characters. The most famous of these is Christy Mahon, the "Playboy of the Western World", a young man who combines the golden tongue and moral defects of the stage Irishman almost to definition. In a quarrel with his father he has hit the older man, taken him for dead, and run away. On his travels he has found that the girls of the west to whom he told this seamy exploit are deeply impressed by a man who "has killed his da". He takes full advantage of their welcomes, embroiders his account till his adventure seems to match one of Hercules', and sets out to enchant the publican's less impressionable daughter Pegeen Mike. His speeches are part of Ireland's poetry, marrying the merits of two languages. "It's little you'll think if my love's a poacher's," he says to the demurring Pegeen, "or an earl's itself, when you'll feel my two hands stretched around you, and I squeezing kisses on your puckered lips, till I'd feel a kind of pity for the Lord God is all ages sitting lonesome in His golden chair."

Virtues and Vices

Cristy is a liar, a braggart, a coward. He never killed his father; just stunned him with a shovel. Yet he talks like a poet, and that is what makes him an Irish hero. Talk is Irish life's richest ornament, even when it involves slight distortions of the truth. The stage Irishman is not scrupulously honest. On one side he is too kind-hearted. He hates to say what his listener would not like to hear. This is why he will not say, in answer to your inquiry about a journey, that your destination is a complicated, mainly uphill walk of three miles. He will say it is scarcely more than a mile and will take you ten minutes, sure to God. It is usually claimed that this desire to please comes down from the old landlord days, when it was prudent never to upset one possessed of the power of raising rents and eviction. But it is also likely to stem from an innate sensitivity in the Irish psyche; a native Celtic delicacy of feeling which, it might be argued, gradually infected many of the Anglo-Irish landlord class, so that they too became markedly different from the English.

This delicacy goes further than tact. It embraces imagination, a consideration for the convenience and emotions of others. In a bus or waiting-room where several are seated, it is delightful to notice how readily — much more so than in England or America — feet or legs are moved out of the way of a person passing by. The instinct is to calculate the other person's needs. The rituals of meeting and departure still retain some of the courtliness of old times. Ingenious conceits transfigure bald and possibly offensive statements into nicely exaggerated kindness. The lad who stays late in bed may find himself described not as lazy but as one who "sleeps slowly". The garden owner may invite you, with a diplomatic reversal of usual reasons, to his garden: "I want my roses to see you." And the man on the bird shoot less fortunate than him we met earlier, may be told yes, he shot well: it was just that the good God was very merciful to the birds. If these are lies they are surely virgin white.

Tact, whimsy, eloquence and the curlicues of his logical processes enable this fictional Irishman to get away with his vices. He treats time cavalierly. He is late by minutes, hours, a day or two. He will prolong lunch with an inflow of alcohol until, it being too late for anything else, he may as well start the evening's relaxations. The man that made time, he says, made plenty of it, and those who have waited for him feel they should perhaps have been more philosophical. They feel disarmed. Tomorrow they will be kept waiting again, but without anxiety. The day after they will parry his lateness with their own. They will learn also, if they are wise, to do without the direct answer to their questions. It is possible to see this principle in physical terms. Two objects coming at each other from exactly opposite directions will hit with heavier impact than if the approach is at an oblique angle. So with dialogue, in stage Ireland. A direct question put to the Irishman causes him a slight shock, and has his mind scurrying through boltholes for the indirect, deflectionary, possibly comical reply.

The Englishman and the American — even the Irish American — come from a culture where the spread of information by media, education and conversation, is considered sacrosanct. They put a question and want the answer. Questioned, their instinct is to give an informative reply. They may, if they are observant, notice the effect on their Irish interlocutors of outspoken queries and responses: a slight unease, a patient melancholy. They may learn to leave as much as possible a mystery. A wily and waspish observer of the Irish scene, Honor Tracy, wrote somewhere of "the swimming sensation in the head, familiar to all who search for truth in Ireland." And elsewhere: "There is nothing like a knowledge of the orient to prepare one for Ireland." Of all oriental practices, the tea ceremony, with its rituals, caked smiles and avoidance of spontaneity, would perhaps be the most useful rehearsal.

The real Irish will, we have seen, often be at pains to explain that there is no such thing as the stage Irish. One of the great sadnesses of modern Ireland is that, having thrown off English rule, it tries to eliminate all trace of it. All too many Irish cannot look at the magnificent domed Custom House or the slightly irregular brick terraces of Merrion Square or the surviving Palladian mansions of the counties round Dublin without seeing in them the cold sneer of the 18th- and 19th- century colonial English; consequently they go to great lengths to substitute the featureless towers of steel, concrete and glass by which future generations will distinguish our era. The stage Irishman is another target of these militants. They see in him, along with the charm of his blarney, something cringing and flattering. They are right, up to a point, to do so. They go on to deny that he ever existed, and in this they are wrong.

The Chosen Race

It is not to say there are not other qualities, incompatible with this controversial character, which are just as typical of the Irish, though less publicised and less pleasing to the visitor. There is, for instance, a certain age-old national conceit, a tendency to exaggerate the merits and virtues of the island and its inhabitants, a quality sometimes known as giantism. The Black Bull of Cooley, a central figure in the finest ancient Irish epic, was huge. Not huge in any normal sense, but of an unspeakable and outrageous enormity. No less than a hundred warriors could take shelter under his massive body, while fifty boys would play games on his back. He was capable of fathering fifty calves in one day, and for good measure all of them would be born the day after. That is giantism at its most gigantic (there are plenty more examples from the literature of similar nature); but if it seldom aspires to such heights, the urge to exaggerate out of self-esteem is seen in various Irish contexts.

From ancient times to the present there has been a tendency for Ireland to regard herself as God's chosen race. The ancient Irish saints appear in old accounts to have had special relationships with the disciples, even Christ himself. St Brigid or Bridget, Ireland's senior female saint, is said to have dandled the infant Christ at her knee. Some accounts almost seem to confuse her with the Virgin Mary. There are claims, serious enough to have led to excavations this century, that the Ark of the Covenant is buried on the ancient royal hill of Tara, outside Dublin, and that a stone which now bears an

An Irish banquet (woodcut by John Derrick, 1581.

inscription commemorating Irish patriots was the very pillow on which Jacob rested his head when he dreamed of a ladder reaching to Heaven.

These, of course, are picturesque curiosities of a kind which every country preserves. But Ireland has something more. Conversations about Indonesia or Africa tend to become about Ireland within a minute or two. Irish objects are upgraded: what others might call ponds or pools are unequivocally lakes, streams become rivers, biggish hills are mountains. Harmless again, but this aggrandisement reached what some see as a dangerous climax in the 1916 Rising, the first harbinger of independence. The leader was a visionary schoolmaster and poet by name Patrick Pearse, who knew well that he and his comrades could not win the battle. But he saw also that defeat and execution would turn them into the martyrs the cause needed. "The Gael," he had written, "is not like other men. The spade and the loom and the sword are not for him. But a destiny more glorious than that of Rome, more glorious than that of Britain, awaits him: to become the saviour of idealism in modern intellectual life." The idea of martyrdom, of being a saviour, of losing the battle in order to win, of working out a divine purpose, hinted at an equation with Christ. The choice of Easter for the insurrection seemed to be trying to achieve for it some of the status and aura of the Passion. It was an explosive formula for a country divided by a species of politics almost indistinguishable from religion. It was also the foundation of the modern Irish state.

Poverty and the Pub

You could visit Ireland twenty times without realising this, since no country has so thoroughly and successfully concealed the harder and gloomier aspects of life. Only in the few parts of Belfast, Derry and county Armagh where sectarian tension is kept high, or in the overcrowded streets of Dublin, where poverty reproduces scenes more suggestive of 19th-century Naples than Ireland at the approach of the year 2000, do the harsher realities of Irish life nakedly intrude themselves. Escape routes change little. There is drink, and the world of the bar, which is its natural home. There is music and song, also indigenous to bars — certain bars all the evening and many more bars at the latest hours of the evening. Bars are the essence of Irish life, though it has to be said there are many who never enter them. Refusing to drink has an honoured place in Irish life, as does Father Mathew, the so-called "apostle of temperance", who early in the 19th century preached against the poison of alcohol, and who still looks down from several statues in his likeness on a community largely heedless of his message. Abstainers today are often members of the Pioneers, or Pioneer Total Abstinence Association, and wear a small Sacred Heart buttonhole badge to indicate this. They require considerable strength of mind. Ireland, where both whiskey (so spelt, unlike Scotch whisky) and Guinness stout were invented, is drinkers' territory.

Laws to do with driving, cost, and considerations of health have changed drinking habits in recent years in Ireland as they have in other parts of the world. But they always did change. That anarchic playwright Brendan Behan, whose death when he was scarcely over forty was due to years of massive overconsumption of beer, put part of the blame for his condition on attitudes among the Irish poor when he was growing up. "Drunkenness was not regarded as a social disgrace. To get enough to eat was regarded as an achievement; to get drunk was a victory." It recalls those Muslims who get unhealthily fat simply to show how rich they are. But there have always been drunks in Dublin, lurching along the streets, cursing the pavements, or some absent enemy, or the tiresome need to sleep before the pleasures of getting drunk can again be enjoyed. "A nose-red city half as old as time," said Oliver Gogarty in parody. On another occasion, bemoaning the loss of the heroic drinkers of his youth, he gave the world a pun of some distinction: "*Où sont les nez d'antan?*"

Probably the Irish drink too much, but there are statistics to show the consumption per head is only a quarter of the French equivalent. But even in their cups they are Celtic. They do not, in the manner of some Englishmen, look on alcohol as fuel for the consummating punch-up in the yard outside. They drink for the intrinsic pleasure, for the lubrication of talk, for a melodic rendering of some old ballad. The only Irish alcohol problem, said a wit, is getting enough of it. And they drink for the sake of company. In other countries the swing of recent years away from drinking in bars to drinking in the home has been pronounced; in Ireland hardly noticed. There is it is true a certain Viking quality about the drinking: a wish to show a grand capacity for the stuff along with perfect control of all faculties. Yeats and some others were despised by hard drinkers. "Bun men", they were called from their preference for tea-shops. (Yeats claimed he only visited a pub once, and after a small drink asked his companion if they might leave.) When the author Brian Nolan was actually dying in hospital a visiting friend poured him the drink he had asked for, a strong gin and tonic. The gin, under Nolan's direction, was almost up to the top of the glass when the man tried to add some tonic. "Almighty God," came the desperate cry from the deathbed, "are you trying to drown it entirely?" On another occasion, better perhaps recalled than witnessed, naked *machismo* was on display. Brendan Behan was far gone, struggling a bit with his words, but managing to tell the first half of some riotous story. Surfeit overcame him. He turned aside, threw up, and then, to the admiring astonishment of his companions, turned back and finished the story.

That was at the Bailey bar, which at the beginning of the century was frequented — many using the private bar upstairs — by writers and congenial politicians. But it was associations with James Joyce (and a rebuilding in the 1960s) which later caused its character to change, for Joyce like Yeats draws pilgrims from all over the world, anxious to tread every footstep the master took. The bars of Dublin in particular have distinct atmospheres and some distinct clienteles: journalists and their hangers-on, barristers, financiers. Some are noted for their music. Others for character of design, furnishings and bric-a-brac. There are some which suggest by the unconscious tangle and trumble of their effects, the dark turned wood, low beams, brass taps on barrels and background frieze of bottles and glasses, that the complexities of Celtic art have here found their modern home. Most have a certain cosiness, an atmosphere of intimacy, which finds its perfection in the name and reality of the "snug" a cubicle with frosted glass windows and highbacked benches in which a small number may confide their racing tips, their market secrets or their love for one another. The air of confidentiality, so flattering to the one addressed, is seen at its most conspiratorial in the pub.

Talkers and Singers

They say the great age of these institutions was in the forties and fifties, when the likes of Behan and the poet Patrick Kavanagh and Brian Nolan alias Myles na nGopaleen strode from one bar to the next, while money lasted, until they could barely walk, and someone willing to repay them a little for the entertainment they provided would load them in a car and take their snoring bodies home. Certainly their humour had edge to it. "You're only a minor poet," someone said to Kavanagh, who was in fact rather more than that, though he would never have said so. A moment's thought gave him his reply: "Since Homer, we all are." And on another occasion a woman he had seen enough of tried to cadge a drink off him. "I've a mouth, you know," she said pointedly. "You have, woman, you have," he broke out, "and it swinging between your ears like a skipping rope." By and large, though, the repartee of the bar loses by repetition outside, but there is enough reported to make claims for this era viable. Not that the principal participants necessarily saw it as we can. Once when Behan and Nolan, without doubt among the most witty and eccentric men of the century, were leaving McDaid's bar, the one was overheard saying to the other "Tis a pity there's no more characters left these days."

Bars where singing takes place regularly are plentiful, and on the increase. The best known in Dublin is the Brazen Head, 300 years old and in its time the meeting place of 18th-century rebels. But a village called Doolin on the west coast of county Clare has in recent years become the Mecca of Irish folk singing. (The classical tradition is much less strong in Ireland, though Handel wrote the *Messiah* in Dublin — in six weeks, and in 1742 it received its first performance in a long demolished hall in Fishamble Street.) In the past Doolin was overshadowed by the nearby town of Lisdoonvarna, a spa town, where middle-aged farmers who had accumulated sufficient savings would go to find wives. Parents brought mellowing daughters and single ladies came, as did professional match-makers capable of drawing up prudent contracts. A season of dances did the rest. Doolin attracted more bohemian elements, among them the writer Francis Macnamara, whose daughter Caitlin married Dylan Thomas, and whose close friend Augustus John came to stay; they all offended local sensibilities by bathing naked in the sea. Little would surprise or offend Doolin now. There have been pop festivals nearby, and the three pubs offer what many describe as "the best crack in Ireland". "Crack" is from a Gaelic word and means a good time; in this case a good musical time.

Not much is needed: seats for musicians, tables for their Guinness (sipped slowly through the evening, and never allowed to run out), players of fiddle, accordion, flute, guitar, penny whistle, traditional pipes, harp, drum — any two or three or four of these. In such gatherings age is of no consequence. The players' hair may be grey, or gone, or glinting chestnut with pigtail at the rear. And the audience will vary likewise. There will be jigs and reels that set old feet tapping, songs that have the hearers humming, set dances with experts springing and stamping and connoisseurs among the audience nodding approval of the finer points. All evening the Guinness will flow. The pub will pay the players a few pounds at most, but nobody's fortune will be made. All are present for love of music and the companionship it fosters.

Such evenings proceed all over the country. In many pubs closing hour comes and the crack continues, sometimes in a back room whose lights cannot be seen by passing *gardai* or policemen. In the bigger hotels, groups of some fame may be on the programme: the Chieftains, for instance, the best known traditional band in Ireland, or the Bothy Band or Planxty, or just one or two of their number. Or it may be the most famous of Irish singing groups, the Dubliners, whose many devotees have watched their bushy beards grow lighter in colour over the quarter century they have been together, singing every kind of folk song from the holy to the bawdy in their nasal, Dubliny, sandpapery voices. Best may be the evening when no public talent is present, only the local builders or woodcutters or boatmen or greengrocer in whom deep draughts of Guinness will release fine tenors or basses and some deeply sentimental, or patriotic, or patriotically sentimental ballads.

Music is one of the things Celts are made of. Delicacy, often masked, is another. And there is a thick seam of humour, best understated; and cunning, and malice, and prudery, and the desire to please, and a curious mutation of natural logic, and kindness, and oriental obscurantism, and an almost genetic sympathy with horses. But the biggest and most important component of the Celt is the capacity for talk. Talking is the natural condition of the Irish, and no Irish person who is neither speaking nor listening to a speaker will seem entirely at his ease. Little village urchins, long overcoats secured at the waist with twine, like their fathers', will confer quietly among themselves when they have played themselves out of energetic games. Their fathers, wrapped from head to toe in tweed and wellingtons, will conduct dialogues as if the world depended on their outcomes, and so adjusting volume that the closest ear, however close that may be, will detect only a murmur, quite unintelligible.

Old women talk with expressive eyes and expressive hands as their own grandmothers talked, and theirs, back as far as Bridget, perhaps, or Deirdre; and the curious thing is that whether or not the textiles they wear are from Irish sheep or chemicals invented the other day, and whether they are sitting on a summer's evening on the doorstep of a north Dublin slum or a jumbo jet winging its way to Alicante, the ancient legacy, the pointed finger, the grasp of the interlocutor's upper arm, the rounded mouth, the furrowed brow — all go on unchanged. Fat priest talks to thin priest, young man to young woman, bus conductor to the bus's occupants in general, and the nation's office workers, on their way to work, male and female, to each other, unceasingly, unstintingly, with richer vocabulary than most of their fellow English-speakers. The Irish have not produced a prodigious number of great composers or artists or sculptors. The essential Irish art-form is talk.

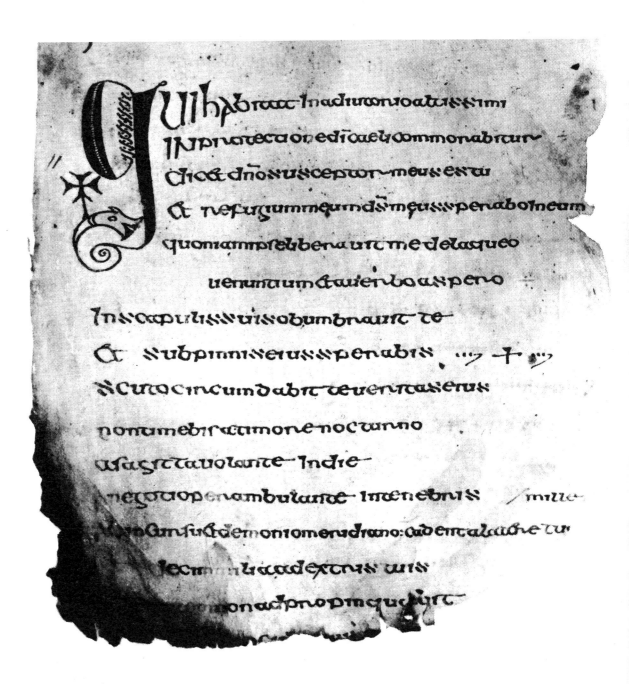

The Cathach manuscript, the oldest surviving Irish manuscript in Latin, believed to have been copied from a book belonging to St Finnian, c. 560.

Ancient Ireland

Prehistoric Times, Myth and Legend

Ireland's remotest past is presented to us in the form of tantalising and imposing clues. Beside the River Boyne in county Meath there stands a group of prehistoric burial mounds of which one, in a fine state of preservation, may now be entered. The layer of white quartz stones which cover its hundred-yard girth seems incongruously dazzling among the quiet greens of the landscape. The visitor walks past threshold stones carved with simple curls that look like neolithic doodles, along a cramped passage to the central corbelled chamber, in which rest three large stone dishes: once — nearly five thousand years ago — the receptacles of the cremated remains of kings. A thin shaft of light enters through an aperture in the wall, scarcely enough to illuminate the scene, except for a handful of days before and after the winter solstice. During this brief interlude, and then only, the sun's rays penetrate the hole and fall directly onto the dish. It is reminiscent of the alignment of stones at Stonehenge, where the rays of the rising sun at midsummer shoot through the centres of two of the megalithic arches. We are left to wonder how much other, vanished accomplishments of these early Irish matched their refined command of astronomical data.

Away on the other side of Ireland the largest of the Aran Islands rises on its south-west coast to a height of 330 feet, then falls in sheer cliffs to the sea. On this summit stand the remains of an ancient fort: three lines of stone rampart and outside them a row of pointed stone stakes, erected presumably to repel cavalry charges. The shape of this fort is semi-circular. The ramparts end at the cliff top, and we are left to guess whether a corresponding semi-circle which would have made the whole thing round, or possibly oval, has crashed with a cliff fall into the ocean, or whether what we see is the full extent of the fort. And to imagine what formidable enemy was thought capable by the builders of arriving from across the water with a force powerful enough to warrant such precautions, and what reward the invader would be seeking in this barren, stony terrain.

Ireland abounds in these prehistoric ruins, not a few of them as grand and enigmatic as these. Prehistory is by definition silent, only seldom provoked by the third degree of archaeology to spill some secrets. Two other kinds of source, neither fully reliable, enable us to piece together a patchy account of the country's fortunes before the arrival of Christianity and the art of writing. One is the huge surviving body of myths and other literature, including a code of law, all of them carried in people's memories until they were written down in medieval times. Although the scribes included anachronistic details folded in over the course of centuries, these manuscripts portray with more or less clarity a way of life which prevailed even before Christ was born. The other important source is the evidence of ancient Greek and Roman chroniclers — rather too ready, some of them, to believe outlandish tales about far-flung realms — along with the knowledge of continental population shifts whose outer ripples affected Ireland.

We know for instance that people reached Ireland about 6000 BC — it was around this time that the withdrawal of the glaciers of the last ice age finally allowed for normal human existence. These were middle stone age men, good at getting around on the water, living by lakes and rivers, eating fish. The new stone age — neolithic — people who arrived about 3000 BC were by contrast farmers, masters of flint, who chipped it into axes to fell large forests and establish pastures and ploughlands. The suc-

17

16. The public buildings of Belfast tend to be grandiose, ambitious, and often quite dull. The City Hall in this picture, dull inside but externally impressive, was built in 1906 at massive cost in a sort of neo-Renaissance style. Statues of various Ulster worthies stand guard, including the Marquess of Dufferin, once Viceroy of India, Sir Edward Harland of the shipbuilding firm, and others less notable.

17. Schoolgirls pass the gates leading to the National Gallery of Ireland. The girl on the right is one of the four per cent of Irish who have red hair, a high national average. Out of sight on the left is Merrion Square, the finest Georgian square in Ireland, noted also (as are other squares and streets) for the elegance of its lamp-posts, glimpsed here.

18. Pro Deo et Rege. . . 'For God and King'. Republican Ireland abounds with relics of the kingdom of which it was once part. Pillar boxes still carry the initials of sovereigns. Numerous institutions remain nominally 'Royal'. In the Chapel Royal of Dublin Castle, once official home of the viceroy and still reserved for state occasions, the trappings of the Catholic Church mix uneasily with the emblems and coats of arms of English royalty and the Protestant aristocrats who deputised for them.

19. The main staircase inside the National Gallery in Dublin. George Bernard Shaw, the playwright whose portrait appears in the centre of the lowest row, left the gallery a third of his estate. It was well endowed before, but in time this bequest put it among Europe's more important collections. The windfall came when the play Pygmalion was adapted into My Fair Lady and began to earn millions of dollars.

20. The outward appearance of many Irish pubs is elegant and inviting. The restrained charm of the black-and-gold here is augmented by the coat of arms with a crown denoting the ancient royal status of the O'Neil clan.

21 and 22. Irish students and other young people are as subject as those of neighbouring countries to whims and fads of style and fashion. The august chambers of Trinity Dublin and the constituent colleges of the National University, just as much as the towns outside, teem with patched jeans, Mohican coiffes and, more rarely, the enigmatic Renaissance grace of this couple.

23. *Curious stone figures in a church wall on White Island in Lower Lough Erne seem to invite comparison with Polynesian rather than Celtic sculpture. Each of the seven is different. A penannular brooch carved on the breast of one figure suggest that the figures are several centuries older than the church, which was built about 1200, and were probably preserved from its predecessor.*

24. *The finest of Trinity College's fine buildings is the 18th-century barrel-vaulted library; surprisingly, the vault is a Victorian replacement of the original flat plaster ceiling. The library is one of four which the Library Act of 1801 entitles to a free copy of every book published in Britain and Ireland. A large new annexe to the library, built in 1967, helps to house the more than two million books.*

25. *The state drawing room of Dublin Castle, with much of the furniture here in the days of the British. The Castle then was synonymous with the pinnacle of Anglo-Irish aspiration. The phrase 'Castle Catholic' referred to native Catholic Irish who rejected the nationalist ambitions of most of their faith and were in all other essentials indistinguishable from upper-crust Protestants.*

26. *A wooden column on which visitors have carved their initials and signs for centuries.*

27. *The domed hall of Emo Court, built in the last years of the 18th century for the first Earl of Portarlington (whose descendants have migrated to Australia) to the designs of the great James Gandon, architect also of Dublin's imposing Custom House and numerous other Irish buildings. A Jesuit novitiate earlier this century, it was bought in 1969 by Mr Cholmeley Dering Cholmeley-Harrison and superbly restored.*

28. In the soft light indoors the consumption of beers, stout and whiskey proceeds; outside, people wait for lifts while an elderly woman wheels away her market stock of apples. Unlikely that much thought goes to the man whose name distinguishes the pub: Daniel O'Connell, whose formidable but quite peaceable rallies forced the government to rescind all the laws which handicapped Catholics in 1829.

29. Students of Trinity College, Dublin, wear much the same gear as students anywhere in Europe or America. Forty years ago Trinity was exclusively Protestant, not because it wished to be but because the Archbishop of Dublin refused to allow Catholics to attend what had been a bastion of the Ascendancy.

30. If this boy is typical of his generation, he will tell you that when grows up he would like to emigrate, probably to America but possibly to England or another Commonwealth country. The chance that he will actually go is not great, but a marked reduction of emigration in the 1960s and 1970s has now given place to a steady increase in the numbers.

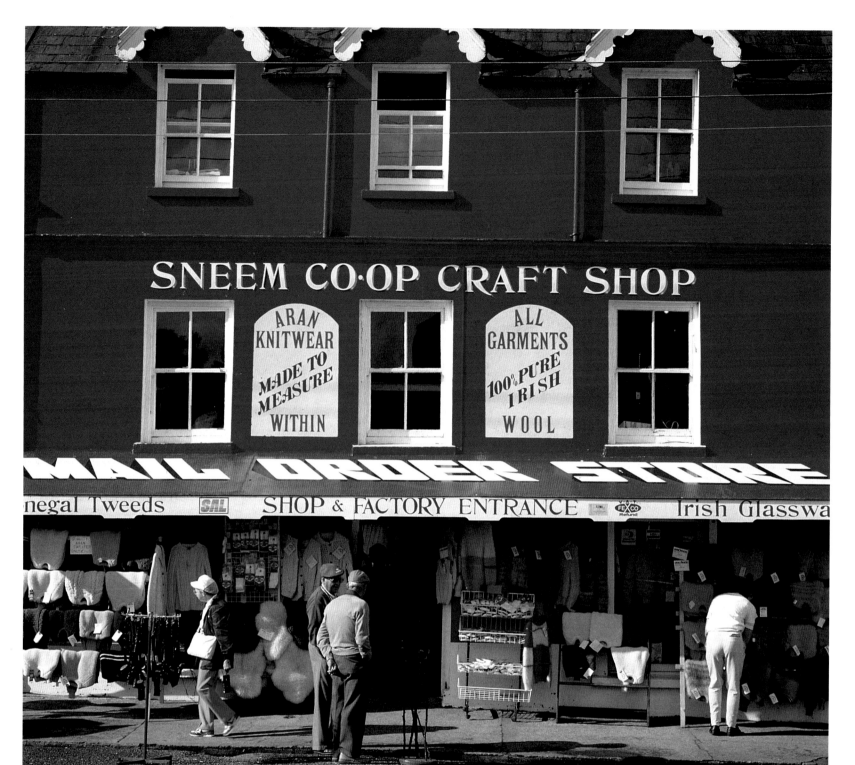

31. *Sneem is a pretty village in a wonderfully dramatic mountain setting on the so-called Ring of Kerry. Most houses go in for bright colours. The vast majority of the goods sold here by the successful Sneem Co-operative show the continuing Irish dependance on the sheep for wools of all kinds.*

32. *Outside a men's outfitters, fitted-out men take life easily. The only anxious expression is on the face of the grey-suited man who has failed to get himself a seat. The prevalence of jackets and ties suggest a Sunday, with mass soon due.*

33. *Pegasus aspires to the sky. There are two of them, in fact, facing each other on the spectacular terraces above the lake at Powerscourt, country Wicklow. Pegasus is the supporter of the coat pf arms of the Wingfield family. These two bronze statues were made in Berlin in 1869. Classical statuary was often employed to add dignity and cultural tone to Ireland's municipal building and stately homes.*

34. *The figure of Erin stands over one of the dying warriors. A modern representation of Erin stanting over one of her dying warriors. Contrasted in style are the arches behind, belonging to James Gandon's late eighteenth century Custom House, which fronts the River Liffey. In Dublino Irish myths and legends are another source of inspiration for sculptors.*

33

34

35

35. George Bernard Shaw's favourite sculpture of himself by the Polish Paul Troubetzkoy stands outside the National Gallery, off Merrion Square, in token of the very large bequest he made to the gallery. Born in Dublin, he lived there till he was twenty, after which he made his home in England, where he died at the age of ninety-four.

36. An armorial Pegasus in stone at Powerscourt, representing the arms of the Wingfield family, whose title, the visvountey of Powerscout, drew its name from their splendid eighteenth century house in county Wicklow. The house bruned down in 1976, but the magnificent gardens remain.

cess of their enterprises released them from the need for constant attention to survival. They took up some of the habits of luxury, created gigantic earthworks, and buried their kings under huge mounds and coverings of bright quartz in such enduring necropolises as the Newgrange complex. Probably they had a priest class versed in astronomy and able to make the observations and calculations necessary for the orientation of these tombs.

By 2000 BC immigrants capable of working bronze arrived, introducing elaborate new designs along with their techniques. Then, around 600 BC, came the Celts. This was a race of sophisticated social structure and formidable military power which had for some centuries occupied much of the mainland of Europe, from modern France in the north-west to modern Turkey in the south-east. In clashes with the emergent power of Rome they inflicted some crushing defeats, and the Romans for their part showed exceptional pride when they worsted the Celts. Nevertheless, Romans were not generally complimentary. They described the Celts' fearful appearance, their shagy locks, the practice of human sacrifice and those mournful nasal intonations which, characterised as "ba-ba", had given rise to the Greek word — subsumed by the Romans — barbarian. However, Roman commentators gave credit to the artistic achievement of the so-called *La Tène* culture of the Celts, their artistic, musical and poetic skills and interests, the rigid hierarchy of their class structure, their mature and complex theology, their strong faith and the formal courtesy of their manners. These were the people who, half a millennium before Christ, introduced the iron age to Ireland, and imposed their arts, language and social patterns on already complicated cultural strata.

So much is history. Myth, as is its nature, has a different story to tell, but it may well spring from the same factual sources. Legends surviving from pre-Christian times (though not generally written down until the Middle Ages) describe successive waves of invasion of Ireland. In these accounts the conquering immigrants usually destroy or exile the vanquished, having in certain cases removed a daughter of the old stock to marry a prince of the new; or else consign them to furtive immortality in the sunless gloom of caves and lake bottoms. The very first settler, Partholon, perished of plague with all his followers. The forces of Nemed who came next were savagely harrassed by the vicious Fomorians, who lived under the rule of their one-eyed king Balor in Tory Island, off Donegal's coast, and to whom the Nemedians were obliged to offer up two thirds of their corn, their milk and their newborn children. Balor's one eye was notable for the kind of picturesque detail to be found all over Celtic myth: it took four men to lift the eyelid, and when exposed, the eye could kill anyone on whom its gaze fell. Failing to defeat the Fomorians, Nemed and his company returned, whence they had come, to Spain, making way for the invaders known as the Fir Bolg. This name offers a tempting link between legend and history, for there seems to be a connection between the word Bolg and the name of the Celtic tribe which Caesar was once in awe of, and which in time gave its name to Belgium: the Belgae. In any event the Firbolg (*fir* means men) were an aggressive tribe, recently escaped from slavery in Greece. They were dark and stocky and tough and inelegant, and in later centuries people claiming ancient pedigrees would always deny descent from the graceless Bolgs. In due course they had to turn their attention to the invading Tuatha De Danann, or people of the Goddess Dana.

The Tuatha were divine (though scholars still vex at the question of whether gods are promoted people or people demoted gods). They had a varied and quirky pantheon, of whom the king was Nuada. Having lost a hand in battle against the Fir Bolg, he was deposed, kings being required to be perfect. A later king, Bres, was deliberately harmed to secure the same result, but in a manner which set an important precedent. A bard, Cairbre, admitted to his chamber, delivered a biting satire on the king's disastrous rule. The words hit Bres like darts. His brow puckered and his face came out in a mottle of boils. The elders declared this an official blemish, disqualifying Bres from the throne, and his reign was over. The power of the word has remained paramount among the Irish, and on certain occasions deaths have been ascribed to it.

Other gods among the Tuatha had quaint qualities. Angus (whose name is attached to the ancient fortress we have visited on Inishmore), being god of love, blew kisses which changed into birds that guarded true lovers. Lugh, the sun god, possessed a spear which made up its own mind, flew independently through the air, and always struck its target. Another weapon, the sword of the sea god Manannan, always killed its master's opponent. The same god's horse flew through the air quicker than the wind. An accomplished wizard, he could restrain winds and warp time. Manannan's sister Finola and three brothers were at the centre of one of the most famous and melancholy of Irish legends, retold by parents to this day. Their barren stepmother, hating and resenting them, changed them by means of a spell into swans, and spitefully told their father Lir that they were dead. In fact she had condemned them by her immutable curse to 300 years on Lough Derravragh in Ireland's centre, 300 more in the channel dividing Scotland from Ireland, and yet another 300 in the western sea. Lir, unable to change their fate, was able at least to have his vicious wife turned into a demon by way of revenge. The children still had to serve out their sentence. By the time of their release, Christianity had come to the country. It was the sound of church bells which broke the spell they were under. Without demur they accepted the new religion, even while they were still in the form of swans. When they changed back to their own kind, it was to become not the children they had been but wizened, bent and white-haired humans.

It is clear that such legends, as they were written by medieval chroniclers, were meshed inextricably with the myths and creeds of other cultures and other ages. Innumerable details are reminiscent of Homer's Iliad, the story of the Greek siege of Troy. The cauldron of the god Dagda and the stone which could tell a real king from a pretender by crying out when he stepped on it appear to have strong associations with legends of King Arthur, the holy grail and the stone from which only a king could remove the sword lodged in it. The god Ogma is clearly linked with a much later method of writing: letters denoted by lines carved on the edges of stones and known as the ogham script. Manannan is related to the Isle of Man. Lir is the prototype of King Lear. Many figures from these pagan days were transposed with minimal changes into high Christian status when that religion was introduced. (There were probably no church bells in the earliest tellings of the children of Lir story.) The goddess of fire, Brigid, was processed into St Brigid, revered in Irish Catholicism above all women save the Virgin Mary, and all mortal men save St Patrick. (She was hallowed in Britain too under the name Bride or Brit or, in Roman times, Brigantia.) These stories are a jumbled mass of clues to the nature and identity of the country's prehistoric inhabitants.

There was another invasion to follow, according to the mythical accounts. About the time of Alexander the Great, the Milesians arrived. It took them a long campaign, during which the Tuatha exercised all their magic and ingenuity, to conquer all their predecessors on the island. The Tuatha were humbled, and forced to find sanctuary in the darkest caverns and burial mounds — or *sidhe* — from which, referred to now as the little people, or in parts of the country as leprechauns, they live their greatly reduced existences, mending shoes, guarding their considerable ancestral treasures, and evading the harm and mischief that humans are capable of inflicting.

The Milesians were the followers of Mil and came from Spain. Mil's son was named Goidel and his wife Scota, and the people who are descended from them are variously known in history as the Scots, Milesians or Gaels. With the Milesians, it is plain, we are returning to the borders of history. It is true that they are forced to fight battles with the established inhabitants in which dark phantoms fly through the air shrieking shrilly and dealing death to the newcomers. It is true that long after their settlement in Ireland heroes like Cuchulain and Finn McCool and their followers and adversaries are accomplishing exploits which can only be explained as magic. All the same, the great gap between legend and actuality is narrowing. Traditional sites of supposedly mythical battles have yielded human bones and the remains of weapons. Accounts of Cuchulain's prowess may show he was more than a man. He could, after all, perform on the point of a vertical spear without piercing his soles, the heat of his body when he took his shirt off would melt the snow for a cubit all round, and in battle he might blow himself into a ghastly distorted shape that would scare off all but the bravest. Still, the campaign which left him, though dead, for ever chief and most beloved among Irish heroes seems to have been a stage in a long and real cattle war between Ulster and Connaught.

Pagan Kings and Celtic Saints

The society represented in the tales of these early times (the centuries either side the birth of Christ) is one that continued well into the historical era, and even, in a few respects, into our own century. It was rigidly stratified. The king of each clan was advised by leading members of the warrior aristocracy and by his pagan priests on the matters which most concerned him: such things as hunting, tournaments, rustling a neighbour's livestock, feasts and the recital of long stories. Below monarch and aristocracy came a group of men of great standing and importance whose distinction lay in their memories and their eloquence. They were bards, genealogists, scribes, jurists, historians, artists. They had not inherited their positions but won them by merit. Below them came the farmers and soldiers, whose management of these more modest matters facilitated all the rest. Below them came slaves. It was a pattern which survived, though in slow eclipse, to the times of Oliver Cromwell, who would smash what was left of it like a wreck against the rocks of Inishmore.

While the last of the pagan kings rode and routed their lives away, Europe had been affected by profound changes. The Romans had spread their rule from Britain to Syria. Christianity had been made strong by its experience of imperial persecution. Following the edict of toleration issued in 311, the religion throve throughout the empire, in cities in the hands of priests and bishops, and in withdrawn monastic communities where monks were ruled by abbots. In less than a hundred years, however, all this was under threat from the incursion of hordes of Asiatics, forced westward by pressure of population.

In 410 Rome, under threat herself, withdrew all her forces and officials from Britain to Italy. Into the gap came the Angles and Saxons. Many of the native British were assimilated into the lower ranks of Anglo-Saxon society. Others fled to the mountainous country of west and north Britain and over the sea to Ireland (just as their Celtic cousins in Gaul fled to Brittany, and in Spain to Galicia), taking their Christianity with them. In some ways no import could have been more out of place in the carefree and irresponsible society of Ireland than Christianity with its stern rules, its placing of the next life in a position of priority over this, and its disapproval of some of life's most acute pleasures. Yet Christianity took root and grew in Ireland like orchids in a stove-house. Within a hundred years of its arrival it brought Ireland to the threshold of its most glorious era, the golden age during which this little country acted as a lifeline from a beleaguered Europe to the plateaux of godliness.

First, though, the religion took to Ireland, and especially in its monastic form. The monastery had some important similarities to the innate social structures of the country, to the tightly controlled little kingships with their high regard for cultural matters. Also, probably, in their consignment of women to subordinate status. King Cormac of Tara, who reigned shortly before this time, is supposed to have described women as "haughty when visited, lewd when neglected, silly in counsel, greedy of increase, steadfast in hate, niggardly with food, quick to evil, eloquent of trifles, tedious in discussion . . ." Whatever it was, opposition, of druids as well as laymen, was soon overcome. The credit for this is usually given to a small group of missionaries headed by St Patrick, a Briton captured as a boy by Irish pirates off the coast of Wales (or possibly Scotland), who after several captive years as a shepherd on the hills of Mayo managed to escape to Rome.

Years more were spent in training, till eventually, ordained bishop, Patrick returned to evangelise the country that had kidnapped him. The mission was tough and uncompromising. It took him the remaining thirty years of his life, from 431 to 462, but there is no suggestion that a whiff of paganism remained when, in the latter year, he laid down his staff and died. To this day the most popular pilgrimage in Ireland, drawing thousands of willing penitents on the last Sunday in July, is the climb to the top of Croagh Patrick, the mountain on whose slopes Patrick the boy may have tended his sheep. Ironically St Patrick's own day of commemoration, 17 March, is vastly more popular in the United States, where it has assumed heavy political colours, than in Ireland.

No age so clearly demonstrates all the facets of the Irish genius as the century or so that followed Patrick's labours. The achievement, as we shall see, was prodigious. It became even more so because of the essentially Irish style in which it was later described, and in many cases picturesquely exaggerated. It is clear, for instance, that the good bishop Eric was tough as rawhide. But when the hagiographers tell us that he daily immersed himself in the cold waters of the River Boyne to recite all the psalms, belief falters even while admiration for the charm of the concept grows. The old blurring of the borders between truth and legend is still there; and even if one could tell the one from the other, we should certainly want to preserve both. The same Eric, needing milk for a child he was fostering, prayed for help. Next morning, and on every subsequent morning for as long as it was needed, a hind came down from the local mountain and allowed herself to be milked.

Such empathy, of nature in man or man in nature, is another of the remarkable features of the age. Again credulity is strained, but in a particular way, led on by the Irish gift for somehow stretching logic to a level which transcends reality yet carries within it a logic of its own. Hundreds of tales come down to us. Thus the good hermit Mochua possessed nothing in life except three creatures: a cock, a mouse and a fly. Each had its duty. The cock crowed at the hour of matins. The mouse served a purpose in a way scarcely improved on till our own day of snooze devices on alarm clocks. After cock-crow it would continue to lick his ear till he woke. As for the fly, its office was to alight on the open psalter from which Mochua was reading texts, to walk along under the words he was reading, and when he broke off to contemplate or pray, to stand motionless, marking his place on the page.

There are accounts of miraculously helpful horses, herons, sheep and doves. A bird drops its largest feather beside a hermit in need of a pen. A deer stands still throughout St Ciaran's church services, to let the saint use his antlers as a lectern. Men in their turn show a sensitive consideration to animals. St Kevin, sitting reading in his cell in Glendalough, chanced to rest his elbow on the sill with the hand upraised. A passing blackbird took the hand for a nest and laid a clutch of eggs in it, while Kevin was too engrossed in his book to notice. When he looked up and saw what had happened, he decided to stay where he was until the last of the eggs was hatched. And so it happened.

The charm had an obverse side. Love of nature as practised by these ascetics

Council Book of Galway, 1632, its fanciful and intricate ornamentation recalling the style of Celtic manuscript illumination of almost a thousand years earlier.

Council Book of Galway, 1632. Courtesy of the National Library of Ireland.

fiercely excluded love of women (which was not in those days forbidden to priests). The same St Kevin had been followed to the dark valley of Glendalough by a girl who had loved him for years. When she refused to go away, he threw her over a cliff into the lake of Glendalough. He does not appear to have been upset that she drowned. St Brendan, later to be called the Navigator, was similarly plagued by an admiring girl. Her suit became too pressing, and one day she jumped up into his carriage beside him. He stood up and flailed her with the carriage reins, and was not bothered by her again.

Monastic Achievements

That there is some symbolic truth even in the most unlikely of these tales seems certain. Poems from the period, and the quaintly evolving Celtic art are strongly related in their fancies, their whimsy, their happy imagery. The most famous artistic product of Irish monasteries is the Book of Kells, dating from the late 8th or early 9th century, which represents the culmination of this ebullience. The ornament framing the illustrations of Christ, the four evangelists and the gospels themselves is a quite unpredictable, zany, sometimes grotesque, often very amusing representation of people, animals, birds, monsters, in a broad spectrum of colours. Again the quirky Celtic invention is evident, working to rules of its own, abounding with imagination. Later, much later, a very Irish style of architecture would evolve, perfectly represented by Cormac's Chapel on the Rock of Cashel, in which a riot of cones and arches and slit windows and pillars and carved capitals and frescoes (worn off now) and gables and interlacings of stone serpents shows the enticing restlessness of Irish composition, even though many single elements can be traced to other cultures.

Meanwhile, in the century that followed St Patrick's death, more solid and less speculative achievement was afoot in Ireland. Monasteries abounded. Their rules were strict, with some shocking punishments for backsliding monks. Intellectual discipline was remarkable too, and many of the monasteries attracted monks from other parts of Europe to study and pray. Undoubtedly some of the foundations — St Finnian's at Clonard, St Ciaran's at Clonmacnoise and others — gained a reputation akin to that of the modern university. Those who passed through them were to carry the torch of their learning not only into other parts of Ireland but all across a Europe benighted by barbarian occupation. St Columba, for example, left his native Derry for the coast of Scotland, where many of the population were of Irish stock. (In fact, the word Scot originally meant Irish. Duns Scotus was Duns the Irishman. And the Scottish county of Argyll gets its name from words meaning eastern Gael: that is, the Irish who had colonised Scotland's west coast.) He founded the abbey of the tiny island of Iona, still in use today. From there monks went south into England and founded the abbey of Lindisfarne on the Northumbrian coast, converting the natives of the region and impressing all with their discipline, simplicity and humility. Undoubtedly, St Francis would have felt at home with these Celtic monks, and it was not the fault of the Irish that a clash of doctrines half way through the 6th century led to their eviction from Britain and disconsolate return to their homeland.

On the continent, there was hardly a town whose Christianity was not fortified by Irish influence. Fearless missionaries founded monasteries, assailed corrupt and heathen monarchies and left them Christian and pious, bullied and cajoled their comrades, and are remembered in the history and folklore of all Europe, from Jumièges in Normandy to Salzburg and Vienna, and from Cologne to Lucca. St Columbanus was perhaps the most energetic of them all. He progressed through Europe in the late 6th century, leaving a trail of new foundations in his wake: Luxeuil, St Gall, Bobbio, and many more. He quarrelled with the vicious Visigothic royal house of Burgundy, daring to refuse blessing to two illegitimate princes besides criticising the ungodly ways of the court, and was lucky to escape with eviction. He even quarrelled by letter with the Pope. *Scotti iracundi* — irascible Irishmen — was a familiar phrase of the period, and it is plain that their dogmatism and self-righteousness must have proved at times intolerable. Not the least irritating aspect of them was the continuation of a trait we have already seen in the pre-Christian Irish: the belief that they constitute some kind of chosen race. St Columba's 7th-century biographer tells that before his birth his mother was visited by an angel who told her: "You will bear a son... one of the prophets of God." A similarly messianic event distinguishes St Brendan's birth: a strange light shines in the sky above, and on the next morning a chief brings gifts, and cows come to admire. Female Irish saints are often credited with properties a little too reminiscent of Mary, the Mother of God.

Nevertheless the achievement was staggering. Many claimed the ubiquitous Irish kept the flames of Christianity alive in Europe during the darkest of the dark ages. Irish prestige still rode high in the year 800, when Charlemagne called a number of Irish monks to Paris to enhance his court's reputation. But by that time the missionary impulse had received a devastating blow.

Before that the travels and daring of some Irish monks had led them on quite different trails. The wish to travel has affected most Irish, and what seems to be an impulse to self-exile continues to the present day when, according to new scholarship, the desire for work or to escape poverty does not entirely explain the continuous phenomenon of Irish emigration, even in the shocking times of the potato famine half way through the 19th century. The missionary impulse is there, as strong today perhaps as in the golden age. But there is and was another wish to explore the unknown, and perhaps to discover those realms of poetic imagination conjured by the fogs and foam-capped billows and golden sunsets of the Atlantic.

St Brendan the Navigator

The personification of this drive was St Brendan the Navigator. He was born in Kerry a few miles from Mount Brandon, which takes its name from his, and which provided him in his boyhood with entrancing and irresistible glimpses of the western sea. (The hermitage he occupied on its summit is maintained, and remains the destination of a pilgrimage almost as popular as that on Croagh Patrick.) After training for the monastic life, he planned a voyage — the year is close to 510 — and set off with a party of monks in a curragh, a boat of skins stretched over a light wooden frame, to find whatever was divine and good beyond the visible stretch of the ocean. The *Navigation of St Brendan*, which tells the story of his journey, became an early medieval bestseller and was translated into at least nine languages.

The travellers have any number of colourful adventures in a journey which lasts in all seven years. They land on islands where tables are spread with feasts, which Brendan knows are the work of Satan. They disembark on an island of shiny surface and, it being Easter, they celebrate mass on it. Leaving, they discover the island is a huge and religiously inclined whale, which will oblige them in the same way on the subsequent six Easters. They come to an island on which stands a large tree, not a leaf of it visible through the great clusters of white birds, who turn out to be the souls of Satan's less culpable companions. The sailor monks go on to visit monasteries, hear heavenly choirs, taste strange and luscious fruits, and, as a climax, to visit heaven and hell, which are arranged in a way that anticipates Dante. From heaven, at a guide's invitation, they carry away a boatful of fruit and jewels.

Demonstrably the story is not in every detail true. It contains numerous episodes which are physically impossible, others which have obviously been pirated from Greek and Roman epic tales. Moreover, the name Brendan suggests a link with a former, pagan giant with superhuman powers. Most interpretations are depressingly negative, one commentator going so far as to assert that the whole description (which never mentions distances or time) could apply to an adventurous day's sailing round Galway Bay. However, there is a theory that St Brendan reached America and was the first European to do so. Geographic features tally with places in the story: the Sargasso Sea, Jan Mayen Island, Greenland, Rockall, the Orkneys. That hide curraghs can make the journey has been proved in recent times. It is known, too, that when the Spanish landed in Mexico in the 16th century the Mexican emperor Montezuma ordered that there should be no resistance. His reason, it is claimed, was that the tradition of a boatload of dark-bearded and beneficent wonder-workers arriving from the east had been passed down in Mexico for countless generations, along with the prediction, made by the magicians themselves, that they would return. The argument makes these magicians Irish, perhaps Brendan and his companions. Dark beards were not found among native Indians, whose chins were generally bare, nor among the blonde Vikings believed to have reached the continent in the meanwhile. Spanish beards fitted the old description. Montezuma, inclined to think the Irish were at last come again, was joyfully confirmed in the belief by his astrologers, and Cortes made his conquest without initial resistance through his physical similarities to St Brendan.

The End of a Golden Age

So Ireland's Christianity, in its heyday, converted the heathen, began a long and honoured missionary tradition, kept alive religion and good learning in a Europe where these were under threat, inspired poetry and art and took Celtic designs to new levels of elaboration, and placed Irish feet on the shores of America before even those of the Vikings. Yet for all this ebullience, the golden age was tripped by a snag of Irish stubbornness over a couple of technical details. Rome had decreed a change in the manner of calculating the date of Easter — always a thorny business based on the positions of the sun and moon. (It is curious that having accepted fixed dates for every other feast day, the Church should have retained the crude device of pushing the celebration back or forward to the nearest Sunday.) The Irish, being remote and insular, either missed or overlooked the change and kept to the old method. They also kept going a method of cutting the monk's tonsure — straight across the head — different to the shaving of a central circle of hair practised elsewhere in Christendom. Ignoring instructions to conform, they were summoned in 664 to a synod at Whitby in Yorkshire to justify themselves. The prosecutors expounded their case. It was not simply a matter of date and haircut. Habits and beliefs that smacked of heresy and sorcery were imputed. The Irish were pummelled by a clever orator sent from the Roman outpost at Canterbury, and after more than a week the verdict went against them. They felt they could not remain in Northumbria, and retreated first to Iona and then to an island off Ireland's west coast.

It is true that their influence was not spent. Young men would continue for many years to come from Europe to the forty-five monastic schools in Ireland, and Irish scholars and monks would be found in positions of influence and authority all over the continent right up to the present. Yet the vigour and devotion of those early centuries of Christianity were never paralleled. The interest and intrusion of aggressive foreigners was soon to resume and, on and off, to occupy the hearts and minds of the Irish for a thousand years.

37. The green sward of Ireland nourishes some of the best racing horses in the world, but it produces fine lines of hunters and work-horses too. They say Irish people badly affected by arthritis often find it difficult to move out of the horse-riding position. As elsewhere, there is a lot of enthusiasm to bring cart-horses back into use and save horrific Irish petrol bills.

38. Many writers have commented on the conspiratorial look often adopted by men in conversation. From the furtive looks of them, these four could easily be passing secrets, and may well be discussing the form of horses racing this afternoon and not wish to be overheard.

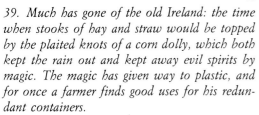

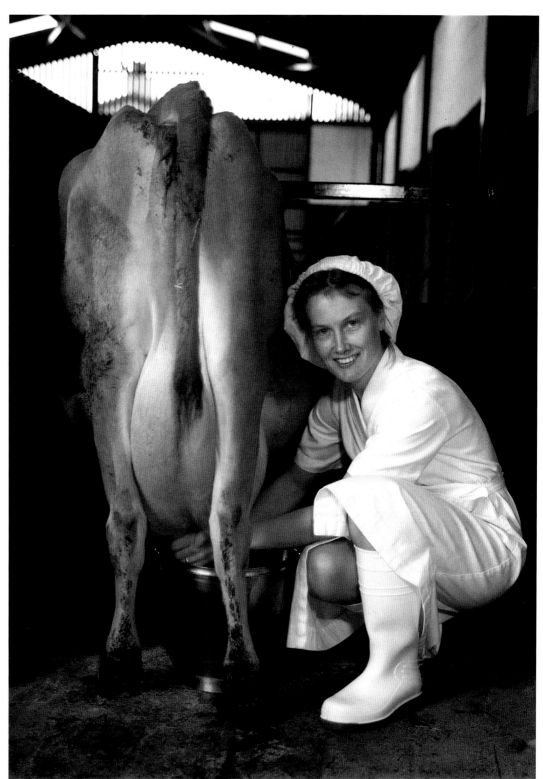

39. *Much has gone of the old Ireland: the time when stooks of hay and straw would be topped by the plaited knots of a corn dolly, which both kept the rain out and kept away evil spirits by magic. The magic has given way to plastic, and for once a farmer finds good uses for his redundant containers.*

40. *Much remains of the old Ireland too: a pretty milkmaid at work in a farm that has not mechanised the process. Most have, so that herds of hundreds can be managed by a single herdsman. Agriculture now accounts for well under a fifth of employment in Ireland. It was a half not so long ago.*

41. Membership of the European Common Market brought enormous initial benefits to Ireland, one of which was the generous grants for refurbishment of agricultural buildings. Water-mills have limited uses in modern farming, although stone-ground flour is rated high.

42. In every European country novelties introduced for the farmer's convenience and economy have often left the country less charming. Aesthetically, the aluminium gate and concrete gatepost on this coastal farm are a hideous substitute for the erstwhile five-barred wooden gate.

43. *Home-baking, whether for family, lodgers or hotel guests, still holds out against the assaults of the commercial firms, sliced loaves and cocktails of chemical preservatives. Soda bread, made with sour milk and raised with bread soda, is popular all over the country. So are all kinds of cake, for Ireland has a distinct sweet tooth.*

44. *Feeding the hens.*

45 and 46. One craft in no danger of extinction in Ireland is that of the blacksmith. Although the motor has replaced the horse in some of its more laborious tasks, the popularity of racing — from international class to the beach races arranged by villagers — and of hunting, as well as the use of horses on the farm, ensures an abundance of horses in need of shoeing.

47. A spruce cottage among the fields and drystone walls that are one of the most familiar sights of Ireland, particularly in the west. The slow, skilled task of building them took place in most cases in the 19th century, when sharply rising population meant frequent division of land among sons. At least it improved much land by clearing it of stones.

48. All over the country, large numbers of houses offer bed and breakfast. Far fewer are approved by the Tourist Boards of the North or of the Republic. Approval is a useful indicator but no guarantee of high standards, and lack of it does not mean the lack of a warm reception, snug beds and a hearty breakfast.

49. A good way to see the beauties of landscape around Killarney is by the form of transport peculiar to the place, the jaunting car. The jarveys who drive them know the area better than almost anyone, and will sometimes offer an outward journey to the striking Dungloe Gap with a return by boat across Lough Leane.

50 and 51. Ireland breeds half as many sheep as pigs and about five times as many cows as pigs, but sheep appear to be dominant in the poorer soils of the west and on the uplands where cattle could not feed, or be sure of finding sure footing in boggy patches. The trouble with sheep is their proclivity to get through any barrier. The varieties of barbed wire, wire netting, twines and strings used for fencing show the farmer is not always successful in controlling their movements.

52. Large parts of Ireland (though by no means all) have escaped the worst ravages of up-to-the-minute farming with all its herbicides and pesticides and chemical fertilisers. One result is ubiquitous clusters of weeds like gorse, nettles, docks, brambles. Another is a rich insect, and consequently bird, population dependent on the weeds. A third is the colourful pullulation of life on a warm summer's day in the Irish countryside.

Norse, Norman and English Invaders

The Arrival of the Longboats

What had been an austere Christian movement became a little more comfortable in the 8th century. Money and treasure came the way of the monasteries, and many of them contained valuable objects they could not properly secure. The armies of the provinces, and individual local kings, were too engaged in old-fashioned feuds and bickering to ensure their safety. The people of Scandinavia, meanwhile, were flexing young muscles. Danes and Norwegians had the fastest and most stable ships in the world, longboats powered by oar and sail. They had steel armour, helmets, axes and swords. They were to prove themselves, for a long period, almost invincible. On their way to carving an empire out of lands bordering the Mediterranean, they limbered up on the coasts of north Europe, or up rivers that gave access to inland loot. In 795, they ravaged and robbed the island of Rathlin, off the north coast of Antrim. Thirty-five years later, the Norse chieftain Thorgest tried to establish his rule at Armagh, a good thirty miles inland. His wife desecrated the holy site of Clonmacnois — right in the centre of the country — by sitting on the high altar and delivering pagan oracles, and in a few years Thorgest was a considerable power in the Irish interior. He claimed sovereignty over all foreigners in Ireland, kept fleets on Lough Neagh and the Shannon lakes, and (perhaps fancying himself like Minos of Crete) demanded as tribute from King Malachy of Meath his daughter and fifteen virgins. The sixteen who arrived turned out to be disguised men. They overcame Thorgest's guard, trussed up the king himself, and drowned him in Lough Owel. But there were more of his kind to come.

These invaders were more successsful and of much greater benefit to Ireland on the coast, where they founded most of the country's main towns: Dublin, Wexford, Waterford, Cork, Limerick. Nevertheless, hostility continued to smoulder and erupt between them and the native Irish throughout the 9th and 10th centuries. From time to time, new Norse arrivals stirred Irish resentment, but it was not until the end of the 10th century that Brian Boru, king of the Dalcassians, a tribe living half way down Ireland's west coast, united Irish feeling and forces sufficiently to pose a threat to the intruders. They, in turn, summoned help from Norse allies who had settled in the Orkneys, Hebrides and Isle of Man.

Brian was a rare figure, a general with political vision and a sense of Ireland's unity. He had usurped the throne of Munster (Ireland's south-western province) and gone on to acquire the title of High King of the whole country. Till then the position had been a cipher, held for centuries by the O'Neill clan. Now Brian made it real, and moulded together the disparate forces of the separate provinces. In 1014, his army met and massacred the Norsemen at Clontarf, just outside the walls of Dublin. Towards the end of the day of battle, however, Brian, an old man now, came to the door of his tent. A Manx chieftain recognised him, rushed at him and split his head with an axe. Brian's dream of a powerful and settled Ireland, of which he saw himself as emperor, were not to be realised. Nevertheless, from then on, Scandinavians who resided in Ireland did so on Irish terms, accepting Christianity and cutting ties with their kin in other lands.

Even so, Ireland had more to suffer from pugnacious Norsemen. A hundred years before Clontarf, one branch of these had successfully settled in France, giving the part they occupied the name Normandy. In 1066, one of their descendants, William, led many others to victory at the Battle of Hastings, winning for himself the crown of England. He planted many of his fellow Normans out of harm's way in the untamed land of Wales, allaying two troubles at once. A hundred years later their descendants were strong, fractious, and impatient.

Conveniently, for them, Ireland produced a Helen of Troy. In 1152, Dermot MacMurrough, king of the south-eastern province of Leinster, had eloped with the willing queen Dervorgilla while her husband, Tiernan O'Rourke, king of the small central kingdom of Breffni, was on pilgrimage at Lough Derg. Though a mature forty-four at the time, she was a great beauty. MacMurrough was used to getting his way. Strong and ruthless, he had once caused seventeen prisoners to be blinded for some minor defiance. This and other cruelties did nothing for his popularity, and in 1166 his vassals rebelled against him. O'Rourke, waiting for a chance for revenge, gave them support. MacMurrough was ousted from his province, and crossed to England. He persuaded King Henry II to give hime leave to recruit an army among the restless Norman overlords in Wales. By 1169, MacMurrough and a doughty force were settled impregnably in a fortress on Ireland's south-east coast, from where he slowly claimed his realm and forged alliances. The following year another Welsh Norman, Richard de Clare, Earl of Pembroke and usually known as Strongbow, joined him with a much larger force. It took little time for the invaders to rout all the local opposition, including the army of the last High King of Ireland, Rory O'Connor, at Dublin. Twelve months later, in 1171, MacMurrough died at the age of sixty-one "without a will, without penance, without unction, as his evil deeds deserved".

What had started as a parochial dispute now took a portentous turn. Strongbow, who had been given MacMurrough's daughter in marriage as part payment for his help, saw that Ireland was at his mercy, and that he had a good chance of making it his own fief. Remembering King Henry, he resisted the temptation.

The king arrived in the country later in 1171, to exact homage both from the Irish and from the newly victorious Normans. He did not declare himself king, assuming

Gaelic chieftains submitting to the deputy of Queen Elizabeth I (contemporary woodcut).

the title Lord of Ireland, but this was a technicality. England had a loose grip on her neighbour, and as time passed the desire to tighten it would grow inordinately.

It was the same kind of harmless insubordination the Irish had displayed before Whitby — over the Easter date and the cut of the tonsure — which assured their submission to England. Popes in Rome had continued to note and frown on the independent line the Irish often took, and to seek ways of bringing them to heel. Indeed, only a few years before, in 1155, Pope Adrian IV had actually authorized the English king to impose his rule on Ireland, in a bull, *Laudabiliter*, which his successor confirmed. It has never been a pleasure to the Irish Church to know that a Pope encouraged the invasion of their sacred land, and brought on them consequences which have burdened and saddened their country for over eight centuries. But they have had opportunity to grow more used to it, for until this century the Vatican frequently took the side of England, or at least of the *status quo*, against Irish attempts to break free.

Already before the conquest a mutual antipathy had existed between English and Irish. The air of patronising superiority shown by the English contingent at Whitby was unshaken five hundred years later. An unsmiling failure to understand the Celt convinced the English that he must be of a lower order of humans, if not of a lower species. Gerald of Wales was one who showed this bias. He was a monk from Wales, a man of literary gifts and the most elevated connections, related to the FitzWalters, Montmorencys, FitzMaurices, De Mariscos, FitzThomases and the FitzGeralds, who together had made the conquest something of a family business, and from whom would spring two of the three most powerful medieval families in Ireland, the Kildares and the Desmonds. As a result of visits to Ireland in the 1180s, Gerald wrote a *Topography* of the country which, though often naive and gullible, is an important guide to the Ireland of the day and shows a deep racial prejudice which was to grow ever more important. "They cannot be said to have any culture," he declares of the people whose piety and scholarship had helped to keep Christian civilisation alive in Europe. They are lazy, he asserts, they avoid work, they wear strange costumes and (perennial complaint about strangers) they let their hair grow long. As he goes on, the eloquent Gerald warms to his theme: "This is a filthy people, wallowing in vice. . . above all other peoples they always practise treachery." They break pledges, oaths and bonds. They go to church to drink each other's blood, and include a rare number of physical freaks due to the high levels of incest and adultery among them.

Throughout the Tudor period, countless rebellions in Ireland were suppressed by force of arms (16th-century woodcut by John Derrick).

Going Native

The curious thing was that everybody who settled among the despicable Irish seemed to want to become one of them. In addition to the military settlers he found there, Henry sent more trusted officials to undertake administration, trade or religious missions, though all were ready to fight in hostile country. An unexpected pattern soon evolved. After a generation or two, the immigrant and his family had become indistinguishable from the Irish. In many cases, male settlers married Irish women, virtually ensuring an Irish upbringing for their children, who would thus grow up almost entirely Irish. For nearly four hundred years this process of "going native" continued. The climate seemed to suit being Irish, but not being English. For England the process was expensive and exasperating, with one ruler after another throwing good men after hibernicised bad. By the middle of the 14th century, patience was running out. At a parliament held in Kilkenny in 1366 under the king's son, a series of repressive statutes was passed, designed to stop the English becoming — as they were called — "degenerate". Marriage between English and Irish was made illegal. So was the use by English of the Irish language, and their adoption of the Irish way of dressing, and riding without a saddle, or of Irish laws and customs. (The Brehon system of law had survived from pre-Christian times and would continue among the Irish for a few centuries more.) Even the Irish model of moustache and the playing of the Irish game of hurling were forbidden. It was an early form of apartheid. It did not work very well.

Other things acted against England's effort to control Ireland. Gone native or not, the powerful Norman families competed and quarrelled with one another and erected the square stone castles whose remains are still seen in every landscape. Some landowners with estates in England as well preferred to spend their time there, drawing rents from their Irish possessions, and starting off the absenteeism which was to help poison relations between England and Ireland a few centuries later. There was, it is true, always an area of relatively strong English influence in the country, centred on Dublin. Known as the Pale, its extent varied considerably, sometimes occupying a handful of counties, sometimes over half the country: mainly the east and south-east and south-western province of Munster. (Not Ulster. It is an irony of Irish history that the home of modern "loyalism" to the English crown held out longest against its incursions.)

Butlers and Fitzgeralds

In the 15th century, when England was distracted by her own dynastic wars, the Pale shrank to hardly more than thirty miles outside Dublin. Beyond it, the degree of cooperation with the English was varied and unreliable (hence the expression, "beyond the pale".) It depended on the dominant families in each area. The Butlers, controlling the old territory of Ormonde, south-west of Dublin, were generally loyal (in time they earned a marquisate.) Other clans were inconsistent. O'Neills, O'Donnells, O'Conors, O'Briens and others were sometimes openly hostile, sometimes so benign as to secure for a son or daughter a royal marriage. But after the Butlers, the most powerful and at the same time mercurial families were the two branches of the FitzGeralds. At the height of their power, the Desmonds were said to control half a million acres of land and a score of castles and grand houses "big enough for the residence of a prince". But the Crown was continually on the watch for overweening behaviour, fearing that those guilty of it might be aiming to make themselves sovereigns of an independent Ireland. Thus Thomas, Earl of Desmond, a man who comes down through the centuries as pious and eminently cultivated, was in 1468 executed by a nervous Edward IV on the grounds of his closeness to the Irish.

The Kildare FitzGeralds were faring better, but times were dangerous. They possessed huge estates, close to Dublin, and kept judicious ties with both the Castle and the native Irish chieftains. Edward IV made Garrett Mor ("Great Garrett") FitzGerald his lord deputy, hoping to recruit his enormous influence, wealth and power to the royal cause. Garrett though roused suspicions. The next king, Henry VII, the first of the Tudors, replaced Garrett with his own Sir Edward Poynings, who was long enough in Dublin to cause the enactment of a bill that became notorious. "Poynings' Law" laid down that no legislation could be initiated in Ireland without the approval of the king and his council in England. The Irish liked to think that the king alone, as Lord of Ireland, was placed above the authority of their parliaments. Not so: from now on an English parliament would be above them too, able to pass or disallow the making of particular laws. The resentment this caused would grow apace.

Meanwhile Henry had learned a truth about Garrett Mor. The earl had not accepted Poynings' regime. He had raised a rebellion in 1495 and among other things set fire to Cashel Cathedral, though without disaster. His arrest followed and he was taken to England and the Tower. When the king asked him why he had put a cathedral at risk, he irrevantly answered that he had "thought the archbishop was in it". A priest, hearing the remark, exclaimed: "All Ireland cannot rule this man!" "Then," Henry is supposed to have said, though it sounds too snap to be true, "he shall rule all Ireland." Garrett was deputy till his death in 1513. In effect he was king, spending many of his later years physically forcing other chieftains into line, and giving much of his fortune to the college at Maynooth and for the acquisition of books and manuscripts. But the family was heading for ruin. Indeed, the 16th century was the last in which the conventions and institutions of ancient Gaelic Ireland could be said to function well.

The English screw tightened. Garrett the Younger (Garrett Og), the ninth Earl of Kildare, spent much of his youth at the English court, pawned as security for the good behaviour of his father, but part of it in fosterage — a conventional practice, predecessor of the boarding school — to a Gaelic king. Henry VIII's chancellor, Cardinal Wolsey, disliked and mistrusted him, and young Garrett bounced between the highest office in Ireland and the Tower of London, more or less at Wolsey's whim. Towards the end of his life, he and his own son Thomas, tenth earl-to-be, were duped by a trick Sophocles might have put to good use. Garrett was arrested for treason on dubious information provided by the family rival, the Butler Earl of Ormond. He was sent to the Tower. Enemies in Ireland spread the untrue rumour that he had been put to death. Thomas his son, known as Silken Thomas from his soft tassels of hair, hot-headedly renounced his loyalty in public and attacked the Castle, home of the administration. He was utterly routed and the following year, 1535, gave himself up in exchange for a proffered pardon. Henry VIII's brand of pardon allowed Silken Thomas to live on for two years. Then, with five uncles, he was hanged, drawn and quartered at Tyburn. The Kildare FitzGeralds were done for. Later in the century, a Desmond FitzGerald's rising offered the army the chance they sought to extinguish that branch also, once and for all, and to step up the settlement of English in Ireland in a systematic way.

The Schism

Things were greatly aggravated in time by Henry VIII's momentous decision to declare himself supreme head of the Church of England and the Church of Ireland, an act which had effects in Ireland quite impossible to enumerate. Quite apart from the insult to God and the Pope which most Irish would have thought it to be, (no lay leader in Christendom had ever been head of a Church before), it was the step which, above all others, made impossible in Ireland a certain bond between landlord and tenant that was able to exist and develop in England. There, whatever differences, resentments and exploitation existed, the master and his family and all his workers and their families bent their knees to the same God under the same roof at least every week. There was common ground and a channel of access from one to the other. In Ireland this was not to be. Here, the master and his dependents would continue for centuries to speak a different language, and worship what were, in effect, different Gods in different churches. Perhaps even more damaging to the chance of harmony, the squire had no necessary contact with his dependents' priest. For his part, the priest had every reason to begrudge the attitude shared by the squire and Protestant parson to his own faith, contemptuously dismissed as papism. Gradually the parish priest (though usually not his superiors, the bishops) would become a focus of resentment and at times open hostility to the ruling class, and there are many who would argue that priests, particularly those of the teaching orders, still fan the flames of sectarian division.

The Tudors, in the person of Henry VIII, inflicted the wound which would never heal. After the declaration of supremacy came the pillaging and desecration of the monasteries, the public burnings of relics (including what was thought to have been both Christ's staff and St Patrick's crozier). Now, in 1541, Henry had himself declared King of Ireland — the first English monarch to do so. And he revived an old policy to strengthen that position, the process of "surrender and regrant", whereby an Irish chieftain was encouraged to surrender his lands to the Crown, knowing that they would be given back to him straight away as a royal grant. Royal authority was strengthened. Gaelic authority was knocked down, for what was overlooked was the understanding in traditional Irish practice on which a chief held land: it was his for life only, and when he died it would go to the newly elected leader, not to his personal heir.

Tudor Colonisation

A few years later, compounding the offence they had given, the English began to put into effect the policy of plantation. Here was another irony. Plantation, which to most seemed like plain robbery of the land, was carried out under a Catholic, for Henry's elder daughter, Mary, was now on the throne. The pretext of recent rebellions was used to assign what are now the counties of Leix and Offaly to English settlers. (The same counties were known up to Independence as Queen's county and King's county, the monarchs referred to being Mary and her husband, Philip II of Spain.) The plans were not rigorously or thoroughly carried out. Irish natives ordered to leave their homes and resettle in the far west hid for a while and returned. Still, the English were settling in larger numbers than ever before and the trend would continue. Queen Elizabeth planted Munster — or a large part of it — from 1586 on, and elsewhere continued the attempt to break up and exterminate the great Gaelic families. Gaelic leaders resisted, and some tried to enlist the support of France and Spain.

The 1590s saw the most intense efforts on both sides. The English were practising naked colonialism; the Irish fighting back with inadequate forces. Two northern chiefs, Hugh O'Neill, Earl of Tyrone, and Hugh O'Donnell of Donegal, kept up sporadic warfare throughout the decade, helped by the incompetence of the Earl of Essex, the queen's favourite, the failure of whose campaign in 1599 was partial cause of his subsequent execution. His successor, Lord Mountjoy, was by contrast coolly efficient. He beat the Irish and a force of Spanish (an insufficient gesture on Philip II's part) in the south at Kinsale, and by 1603 had forced O'Neill's submission. O'Neill and O'Donnell and numerous of their Irish supporters ended their lives in frustrated continental exile,

O'Donnell perhaps poisoned by an English agent. Their departure from Irish shores became known as the Flight of the Earls, and gave rise to many ballads and tearful memories of a Vanished Ireland. New men arrived from England to take their place, of whom Sir Walter Raleigh was a glittering example.

This Renaissance polymath, the poet-courtier who laid down his cloak in the mud for his queen to step on, who carried on the courtly ways of the days of chivalry, founded the first European settlement in America, explored for gold in South America, and wrote the first world history, this man had yet another side to him. At the siege of Smerwick in 1580, the English besieged a force of several hundred Italians and Spanish, sent to help the final Desmond rebellion. The foreigners, outnumbered and starving, surrendered. Once out, they were massacred. Raleigh was one of the killers. A few years later he was possessed of an estate of some 40,000 acres in the east of county Cork, part of the vast territories taken from rebels. His friend Edmund Spenser, famed for the lyrical delights of his long poem *The Faerie Queene*, wrote a prose work too, called *View of the Present State of Ireland*. In it he advocated the rather unpoetic policy of eliminating the Irish. These were the views of the day, and they were the sort of view successful races tended to hold about those less fortunate. The Spanish, after all, had only recently colonised much of South America, with wholesale destruction of the natives, and the French had been massacring their Huguenots. And hundred of years were still to pass before the Indians of North America, the Bantu of South Africa and the aboriginals of Australia were partially wiped out by European immigrants.

In spite of the deserved Tudor reputation for ruthlessnes, and a marked extension of English power in Ireland during the 16th century, campaigns and plantations had been piecemeal and of mixed success. Even the Flight of the Earls, so often sung as the end of the Gaelic order, was not really such. There were to be a few more "final" appearences of the old order: and the Gaelic language and oral tradition survived strongly into the 19th century and even dilutedly into the 20th.

Protestant Immigration

It was the 17th century which introduced a new thoroughness, opening energetically with the plantation of that most truculent of provinces, Ulster. The departure of the earls with ninety other Irish chieftains had left it leaderless, offering the ideal opportunity for a clean sweep of Protestant immigration. Nearly half a million acres were confiscated, and their Irish residents either expelled or resettled. The tenancies of the land were granted cheaply, in lots of one to two thousand acres, to men who had agreed beforehand to fill their individual farms with Protestants. A number of these came from the City of London, which in return for heavy investment in the programme of plantation was granted both the city and the county called Derry. To mark the change, both were renamed Londonderry, though up to the present time few Catholics have ever used the name, while few Protestants have spoken of Derry. Most of the settlers however were Presbyterians from Scotland. Thus Ulster became a predominately Protestant province, but Protestant in a sense not previously familiar in Ireland. Presbyterians had the customary Protestant contempt for papists, regarding them as superstitious idolaters; but they had no high opinion of the established Church of Ireland either. Standing apart from the two established sects, Presbyterians were dour, industrious, Calvinistic, independent, and enemies of aristocracy, privilege and patronage. Compromise was, and is, a word almost absent from their vocabulary. In a few short years Ireland had been provided with a third religious element, one which was greatly to affect the nation's destiny.

Characters as huge and capable of heroism as the archetypal Presbyterian on the one side and Catholic on the other made the ground as fertile for the growth of myth as the Connaght of Maeve and the Ulster of Cuchulain. A rising against the government broke out in 1641. It followed and was bred by the Ulster plantations, the deceits of Charles I, and the tactless, fanatical efficiency of his minister, the Earl of Strafford, who managed to turn every back in Ireland against him before the king abandoned him to impeachment and execution. The 1641 rising was an act of desperation by the native Catholic population. It spread, and was joined by other interests, notably the "old English". Within a year its leaders had set up a provisonal government in Kilkenny, but it was strained by internal conflict, and the issues were blunted by confusion with those of the English civil war. By 1650 it was going cold. That was the year, though, that Cromwell decided to teach the Irish a lesson. He believed the myths that had been disseminated about the 1641 events, tales of the Catholics' unbridled blood-lust, their slaughter of babies, women, priests. He had two other convictions: that an independent Ireland would always be a threat to England, and that God backed him. On arrival in Ireland in late 1649, he turned to the town of Drogheda, about thirty miles north of Dublin, which had favoured the royalists. After breaking through its defences on his third attempt he ordered every armed citizen dead. Three thousand were executed as a consequence, including the hundred who were burned to death in the church where they had sought sanctuary. "A righteous judgement of God upon those barbarous wretches," he wrote, and went on to repeat the action in Wexford. In a breathless campaign of nine short months, Cromwell made himself the most hated man in Ireland. To this day it would be folly to press too hard the case for his merits in most Irish gatherings.

There are those who wish he had gone further. Had he extinguished the Irish, as other nations eliminated those aboriginals who stood in their way, it is argued, it would all be over but for some pious reflections; and Ireland would be a harmonious part of a United Kingdom. Be that as it may, Cromwell's contemporary Sir William Petty, compiler of the first scientific survey of Ireland, had a better and infinitely more humane way. Thousands of Cromwell's soldiers were settling in Ireland on land given as payment or reward for their services. Petty could see what would follow. The soldiers would marry Irish girls, who would be only too happy to wed outside their family Church to gain security, but would rear their children in Catholic, Irish ways and observances. In a generation or two, the English loyalties of the Cromwellians would be forgotten, the whole strategy a failure. Change it, urged Petty; take 20,000 Irish girls and settle them in a sprinkling over England. Replace them with 20,000 English — the prostitutes of Manchester would make a start. The new generation would be unshakably Protestant, and in such numbers that they might in time outnumber the papists. Petty's rewards for his various services to the government was a grant of some 15,000 acres in Kerry, but his plan for reconstituting Irish motherhood was discreetly ignored.

William of Orange and the Battle of the Boyne

So religion stayed at the heart of Irish problems. Plots — some real, some concocted — kept English distrust of popery on the boil, even while the dying Charles II secretly embraced the religion on his deathbed. His brother, James II, succeeded him. Openly Catholic, James tried to reconvert the nation to its former faith. He found more friends in Ireland than England, and rewarded them by turning all the top jobs of Ireland over to Catholics. An awkward rearrangement of authority was well under way when, in November 1688, James's brother-in-law, William of Orange, landed in England with

53. The Chuch of Ireland cathedral of St Finbarr is on the site of the monastery founded by Finbarr around AD 600 and said to be the beginning of the city of Cork. The saint was famous for his foundations and teaching (though legend, possibly confusing him with a saint of the same name, has him riding a horse across the Irish Sea to convert the Scots). The cathedral, built during the 1870s, was designed by the florid and fervid William Burges.

54. The Celtic cross, with a ring of stone encircling the crossing of the beams; the elaborate battlements along the top of the nave and transept walls as well as of the central tower; the polygonal tower at the north-west corner of the central tower — all are distinctively Irish architectural features.

55. Until the 1920s and aftermath of independence, the Anglo-Irish lived, owned property and wielded considerable influence throughout Ireland. The new state's birth pangs sent many to England and elsewhere, cutting their ties with the land their forefathers had occupied maybe since Cromwell's day, maybe longer. Their houses and their churches often fell into disuse and ruin, and thousands of gravestones cover remains of no interest or meaning to those who live nearby.

A stone slab at St MacDar's Island (county Galway), with carved ornamentation on front and back.

56. In the crypt of St Michan's church in north Dublin lie the astonishingly well-preserved remains of some very old, possibly medieval burials. One of the figures here is supposed to have been a crusader. The state of their skin and bones is attributed to the moist atmosphere maintained by limestone walls. Exposing them in this manner is not in keeping with Christian doctrine.

57. A pile of temporary crosses, to be used for a few months while the earth in new graves settles.

58. The tall and elaborate doorway around the entrance to the Church of Ireland cathedral of St Brendan the Navigator, built over the site of the saint's burial. St Brendan, who flourished around 500, is thought by some to have been the first European to reach America. The present building dates from the late 12th century and the doorway is one of the masterpieces of Irish Romanesque style.

59. *A Catholic priest reads the mass. Ireland remains a deeply religious country in which a person's religion is the first thing others want to know about him. The Republic is essentially a Catholic state although it aims at equality for members of all religions; and no less than two of the state's five presidents have been Church of Ireland.*

60. *A rather saccharine statue of the Virgin Mary holding the baby Jesus, above a number of candles lit in her honour. The Irish are not always strictly in line with Vatican doctrines of Catholic Christianity, and have in the past held to accord more honour to the Virgin than her status outside the triple godhead warrants.*

61. *A priest brings the mass, and the sacrificial wafer which according to Catholic doctrine of transubstantiation actually becomes the body of Christ, to a woman not well enough to make the journey to church.*

62. *The priest is often the most important man in the parish, with enormous spiritual and moral authority. In the thirty years since Pope John's second Vatican Council, the Irish priest has had more adapting to do than most, the Irish Church having in general been less liberal than most others and often a worry to the Vatican on that account.*

63. *Blarney Castle, near Cork, was originally a McCarthy property. The Blarney stone helps to form one of the machicolations just below the roof. Those who kiss it are supposed to be rewarded with great fluency of colourful speech, though few will vouch for the slightest difference of articulacy in those who go through the ritual.*

62

63

64. Ever since the arrival of St Patrick to convert the pagan natives in 432, Christianity has played a dominant role in the history of Ireland and left an indelible imprint on its landscapes, their natural beauty enhanced by innumerable churches, monasteries and convents. While the most ancient are now mostly picturesque ruins, religious faith burns as fiercely as ever. Ireland remains, as it has been for centuries, one of the major sources of clergy for the Catholic Church.

65. *Round towers, tall and thin, and dating from the 9th century, are found all over Ireland in various states of preservation. One of their functions would seem to be defensive, for the doorway is always some feet off the ground, reached by a ladder which could be drawn inside after the monks were safe. The period of their building coincided with the age of Norse raids on the coasts and up the rivers of Ireland.*

66. *The Gallarus Oratory, on the Dingle Peninsula, one of the long fingers of county Kerry stretching into the Atlantic. Dating from about the 8th century, the oratory is one of the most perfect survivals of its time. With only a slight sag in the roof to show its twelve centuries, the skilfully corbelled building is not far from dozens of smaller, 'beehive' cells, possibly used by individual anchorites in early Christian times.*

67. A High Cross and Round Tower (incomplete), two individual features of Celtic architecture. These are at Clonmacnoise, the monastery founded by St Ciaran on the banks of the Shannon. These crosses, richly carved with biblical scenes, may have served as visual aids for monks giving lessons on the Scriptures. The round towers were possibly a Celtic equivalent of minarets, used for summoning the faithful to prayer.

68. Christ Church Cathedral, Dublin's oldest building, founded by Danes in about 1040 but restarted in 1172 on the existing plan, epitomises the city's history. Strongbow, leader of the Norman conquerors, is buried here along with countless later luminaries. The rational 18th century allowed it to decline; a Victorian distiller had it renovated to its present state. The 1980s have lessened it by placing ugly municipal office blocks nearby.

69. St Finbarr's Cathedral, Cork, seen from the bank of the River Lee. William Burge's exuberant designs for the cathedral and other buildings, along with the riots of fantasy in some of his internal decoration (notably at Cardiff Castle), show that he was to have an unlikely influence on the young Walt Disney.

70. The Calvary at Slea Head on the Dingle peninsula in county Kerry. Slea Head is the westernmost point of Europe, so this must be the nearest European sculpture to America. The word Calvary derives from the name Golgotha, scene of the crucifixion of Christ. The word means skull, and some accounts say Adam's skull was buried at Golgotha.

71. *St Ciaran's foundation at Clonmacnoise, one of the most famous monastic schools of the 6th and 7th centuries. The remains include two round towers, one of which is seen above, two high crosses carved with elaborate relief scenes, and the remains of various chapels and monastic building, all set in the magical serenity of flat lands bordering a bend of the River Shannon.*

72. *The round tower and so-called St Kevin's kitchen at Glendalough in county Wicklow. St Kevin came here alone in the year 545 and lived in solitary piety beside the two lakes of this spectacular valley. He had a Franciscan way with birds and animals, and many stories are told of his kindness to them. The surviving buildings, sometimes restored, date mainly to the 9th century.*

73. *The Causeway School at Bushmills, home of
one of the most famous and longest established of
Irish whiskeys. The school was endowed by the
MacNaghten family, prominent landowners in
the district, one of whom was appointed agent in
Kabul after the British invasion of 1839. His
murder by Afghans signalled the hopeless
prospects for the occupying force*

74

74. *A Northern Irish church and graveyard. The Church of Ireland has made a significant contribution to the Anglican Church, having produced a number of strong, evangelical bishops. One woman who left her mark was Cecil Frances Alexander, wife of the Primate of Ireland, who wrote a number of the most popular hymns, including* Once in Royal David's City *and* There is a Green Hill far away.

75. *As well as little glass-encased shrines and grottoes scattered all over Ireland, some substantial and conspicuous patches of land are turned over to the honour of the Blessed Virgin Mary. According to scholars, the early Church, following on from the Jews, gave little reverence to the Mother of God. The Celts, among others, had in pagan times worshipped female as well as male gods, and greater recognition of Mary by the Church could ensure greater loyalty to Christianity. The statue here, at Ballinspittle in county Cork, has recently been claimed to move miraculously.*

the connivance of key grandees. He took little time to bring the English over to his side, and it was clear his cool, imposing progress would before long bring him to Ireland. Opposition to James had come from Londonderry and Enniskillen, the only towns left under Protestant control. The previous December, the governor of Derry had wished to give in to the Jacobite forces, but a group of young apprentices had seized the town's keys and locked the gates against the Catholics. (Every year the Protestants commemorate the action with a march and — till recently — by burning the governor's effigy.) Much more opportunity for valour was to come. In April 1689, they closed the gates against a determined effort by the Jacobites to take the town. The siege of Londonderry followed: 105 days in which the Rev. George Walker's silhouette was seen vividly exposed on the city walls as he exhorted 30,000 townspeople to endure hunger, thirst, disease, the death of their families and friends, and the eating of dogs and cats and candle tallow, for the sake of survival; until the good ship *Mountjoy* sailed up Lough Foyle in the face of Jacobite salvoes, broke the besiegers' boom, and unloaded its bounty of food and other supplies, thus preserving th Protestant city and accomplishing an exploit as vivid in the minds of Protestants today as ever it was.

The decisive battle took place a year later, in 1690, beside and in the River Boyne. Again there was that painful irony that has taught the Irish to trust in no-one but themselves. William came not only with a large English and continental army but with the blessing of the Pope, the Holy Roman Emperor and the king of Spain, with whom he was allied against France, James's main supporter. At the Boyne, in July, William's troops, outnumbering James's by nearly three to two, trounced them. James fled, leaving behind the unfair impression of a self-serving dolt. He was congratulated, they said, on having won the *retreat* at high speed. James's "weakness, imbecility and bigotry," wrote a respected historian two centuries later, "lost him a crown." Another myth had crystallised. Not of the brightest, but stubborn and steadfast, James was no fool and capable of heroism. Everybody, however, was against him. Hearing the result of the battle, Pope Innocent XI had St Peter's illuminated and drank a toast to William.

A couple of battles remained to be fought, and a couple of memories to be passed down for the reverence of future generations. At Aughrim, a sequence of logistical faults led to the death of thousands of Irish. At the siege of Limerick in 1691, the most romantic of Irish generals, Patrick Sarsfield, inspired his men to spike the English guns, commandeer English supplies in daring nocturnal dashes, and endure a month's siege before the inevitable surrender. Terms were granted. The Irish soldiers were to depart unmolested to exile in France. Catholics who chose to remain would have the rights they had enjoyed in previous reigns guaranteed. Fourteen thousand men left Ireland in the days that followed, a mass migration that came to be known as the Flight of the Uild Geese. In France, the refugees were to form the Irish brigade, and in years to come would inflict signal defeats on the English they were unable to worst at home. Sarsfield himself died of wounds two years later at the Battle of Landen. Seeing the blood flow he lamented: "Oh that this were for Ireland." It was a kind of epitaph for the wild geese.

The English did not keep their bargain on the matter of Catholic rights. Ireland was now theirs — as it seemed to them — to shape and mould to Protestant perfection. In striving for this ideal they were, during the course of the next century and a half, to evince the utmost callousness and cruelty, and at the same time to create a veneer of decorous living which, bringing together characteristics of both Irish and English genius, was an adornment to civilisation.

The Age of the Ascendancy

Jonathan Swift and the Anglo-Irish Repression

Far from the great ships of state, little skiffs and wherries floundered about in contrary currents, trying to find their bearings and row to safety and affluence. Ten years after Cromwell, and just after Charles II had been placed on his throne, three brothers in Herefordshire by the name of Swift heard of the openings in Ireland. So much in that country needed repair, so much administering, that there were jobs galore. They were soon employed. One married a distant relation of the poet Herrick, but died just before the birth in Dublin of his son Jonathan. The boy went to school in Dublin and Kilkenny and finished his education at Trinity College, Dublin, which had been founded for Protestant education a hundred years before. All his blood was English. All his education was, if not Irish, certainly in Ireland. He would call himself Irish, but it was with great reluctance, after a frustrating involvement with the political world in London, that he settled for a position in the Church of Ireland. "I am condemned to live again in Ireland." He became dean of St Patrick's Cathedral in 1713, and remained so until his death over thirty years later. During that time he became the beloved champion of a people he despised.

All the same, Swift had a strong sense of justice. When he looked at the lives around him his fury erupted. "*Ubi saeva indignatio. . .*" begins the epitaph above his grave in St Patrick's; "Here he lies where bitter rage can no more tear his heart." (Yeats called it the greatest epitaph in history.) In everything he saw folly, selfishness, humbug, the cardinal vices. Exposing this was his motive in writing his most famous book, *Gulliver's Travels*, intended not for children, who love it, but for adults who might see the point of its barbs. He looked at England and at English motives in retaining control of Ireland; they were not directed at the improvement of its people's lives, or their security or moral standards, but at keeping them from being a nuisance or an enemy's ally, while at the same time stopping them from becomming commercial rivals. Swift devised a slogan that cut through to the matter's heart: "Burn everything British but her coal." He looked at the native Irish. He wrote "Whoever travels this country and observes the face of nature, or the faces and habits and dwellings of the natives, will hardly think himself in a land where either law, religion or common humanity is professed." Then he composed one of the most telling satires in the English language, the *Modest Proposal*, in which he sarcastically proposed that starving Irish children should be systematically fattened up, slaughtered and sold as food for the rich. As an extra source of profit, the skin, "dressed, will make admirable Gloves for Ladies, and Summer Boots for fine Gentlemen."

It was not love of the natives that spurred him to such mordant irony. He did not love them. He constantly expressed his contempt for them, and at his death left money to endow a lunatic asylum:

> "To show (he wrote) by one satiric touch
> No nation wanted it so much."

(St Patrick's, the hospital in question, is a respected psychiatric unit today.) He never identified himself with the native Irish. When he used the word Irish of himself he meant, as others of his kind did, the so-called Ascendancy, the Protestant middle class which occupied every post of influence and significance in the country, that powerful minority which came to be known as the Anglo-Irish to English observers, as English to the native Irish, and as plain Irish among themselves. The 18th century saw the term Irish greatly magnified in complexity.

It was a stage in the creation of modern Ireland. Native Gaelic culture was now all but extinguished. Those of the natives who could had left for foreign lands, or abandoned their Irishness, and often enough their religion, to become, or set themselves to become, English or Anglo-Irish. Names preceded by O or Mac and bulging with Gaelic th's and gh's and soft diphthongs were slimmed down to the simpler phoneticism of English. Peasant ways and attitudes and practices, nostalgically regretted in our day, were gladly jettisoned by those who were kept poor by them, who saw them as deadwood holding them back and found the means to escape. A handful of old-style bards lived on, some maintained by the last of the Gaelic courts as official story-tellers and genealogists. And the priests kept education going, at outdoor "hedge schools", where these illegal activities were unlikely to be discovered. For the Gaels were being squeezed out of existence, their culture impoverished, their religion and priests acquiring the character of stubborn resistance.

A shapeless body of legislation known collectively as the Penal Laws was intended to make life all but impossible for Catholics, depriving them of rights, land, horses, pride. The Irish had always evoked the scorn and hostility of many English, much of it based on malice and myth. Now a new character was emerging, shorn of self-respect, forever ready to perform. In certain Irish faces, from this time on, proneness to smile, to confess, to slip into subservience, to turn a threat into a joke, began to bring their own lines to cheek and eye-corner, and create a characteristic of Irish looks. These were the only expedients left to the Irish: these and terrorism. Here and there, for most of the century, gangs of youths — they called themselves Whiteboys — roamed the countryside attacking livestock and buildings by night. That was another trend, made perhaps inevitable by circumstances, which would survive into our own times: the dangerous propensity to take up arms to stress a point of view. The superficial wish to please and the deeper wish to fight developed together. So everything typical of the Irish involved some measure of secrecy. The diminished Gaelic world of this period is often referred to as the hidden Ireland.

Living like a Lord

Conspicuous Ireland was Anglo-Irish Ireland, with English blood in its veins, like Swift's, but generally with views diametrically opposed to his: oppressive, insensitive, uncomprehending. However, dilute with pretence and corruption, and trying to staunch the instrusion of the English government while pursuing their own ambitions in their own dominion, they were sharply inclined to bungle and compromise. Where they succeeded, and left a mark still evident throughout the country, was in the great game of grandiosity. In a sense, having usurped power in Ireland, the English added insult to injury by using it as a bottomless dressing-up chest, full of costumes to try on. They dressed up in fine Palladian mansions and lavishly landscaped parks (though not by the voguish designer Capability Brown, who replied, when invited over by the Duke of Leinster, that he had not finished England yet); and when taste changed, they dressed up in battlemented and turreted castles, and thrilled to a Gothic *frisson*. They dressed up in names: stolen Irish names and ringing Norman names and inexplicably hybrid names that carried a flattering ring of a knightly, pagan past: titles like Talbot de Malahide, Clanrickarde, Mounteashel, Stuart de Decies, and house names like Velvetstown, Castle Freke, Byblox, Castle Mattress, Ballysaggartmore, Castle ffogarty. They made up new names for their houses, prefixing them sometimes with an aggrandising "Mount" or "Castle": Mount Shannon, Mount Herbert, Castle Oliver; and they made up ringing names from their own or their wives' names, like Bessborough and Annesgrove. In their passion for theatrical adornment they tended to overlook the tedium of accuracy and historical foundation. To match their Gothic crenellations, they changed their names, without regard for authenticity, from plain English to antique Norman, Mullins to De Moleyns, Power to De la Poer. Typically, where there had been nothing but scrub and fields the Adair family built a house and a church and invented a parish, conjuring the spurious name Rathdaire for it. (Just as typically, they are long since departed, leaving no trace.)

Servants were ridiculously cheap by comparison with English, and it was easy to live like a lord, if necessary a mortgaged lord. Appearances could be almost everything. Visitors to Ireland are often puzzled by the number of massive pairs of pillars flanking drives which bend and coil in a somewhat transparent attempt to exaggerate the distance between road and front door. There are cases where huge mansions were planned, but all money and credit was exhausted by the building of gates and lodges and an occasional bridge to carry the drive over an arcadian waterfall. On a different front of pretence, squire after squire claimed to be untitled only for reasons of modesty. The king himself, they would insist, had pressed them to take a peerage. "I never yet," wrote a wry observer, "met with a man in Ireland who had not himself either refused honours from the Crown, or was not the son of a man, or had not married the daughter of a man who had been hard-hearted enough to refuse the solicitations of the Government."

To the beholder, the results of this marriage of 18th-century grandiosity with the landscape of Celtic Ireland was often enough heavenly beauty, in some cases still visible today. The palatial balustraded façade of Castletown House, flanked by its twin pavilions, is still there, once home of the Conolly family, now headquarters of the Irish Georgian Society. Tom Conolly, the builder, seems to have been indifferent to the skills of the employed artisans. "Frankiney stucco man" is the kind of entry he made in his accounts, referring to the finest plaster-workers of their time, the brothers Francini. But he took care to employ the best. The architects of the house, Alessandro Galilei and Edward Lovett Pearce, and the Francinis themselves, who festooned the main staircase with floating swathes of rococo plasterwork, and the numerous masons and woodworkers and other artisans were unsurpassed in their age.

Dublin's Heyday

Dublin and most other Irish towns have much of the 18th century on display, though time and developers and a tragic, if understandable, wish on the part of some authorities to wipe the country clean of its colonial relics, continue to destroy large sections of the heritage. Dublin's redbrick Merrion Square, built by individual purchasers within strict architectural limitations, recalls the elegance of days when every country landlord would have a town house. The square has a balanced 18th-century congruity about it, yet every house in every terrace has its individuality: small differences of height, fanlight, wrought-ironwork, coping and moulding.

There are grander buildings of the same era: Leinster House, home once of Ireland's premier duke, now of the whole parliament; large parts of Dublin Castle, which in former times was the official residence of the lord lieutenant, and the symbol of imperial rule. Where now heads of state continue to be entertained on rare and solemn occasions by the republic's president, in the days of the British a whirl of elegant entertainment continued through the Season, and every daughter of every Protestant with ten acres to his name came, or languished for want of coming, to be presented to the king of England's deputy at some glorious pageant of a ball. On the north bank of the River Liffey, which cuts Dublin in two, stand two of the most memorable 18th-century buildings: the Four Courts and the Custom House, the city's finest buildings, hugely domed, broad-based and symmetrical, both by the architect James Gandon. Picturing such grace and proportion without the intervals of squalid and charmless buildings that have risen since gives a clear impression of a city that in the 18th century was counted second in Britain after London, and one of the most elegant capitals of Europe.

Such maintained edifices survive the length and breadth of the country, but only a fraction of the number that stood two hundred years ago. Burned, rotted, abandoned, many more remain as timeless ruins, offering through slanting doorways or damp archways glimpses of the ghosts of their heyday.

Great Anglo-Irishmen

The ghosts of 18th-century Anglo-Ireland are by no means all frivolous socialites or people of modest talents parading as something better. The century produced much more than the art and architecture of imported craftsmen. There were soldiers of whom the Irish have always been a foremost producer, more particularly in the 19th century and our own (Kitchener, Auchinleck, Gort, Beattie, Montgomery, Alexander, Templer, Alanbrooke). But the 18th-century output numbered among them the Duke of Wellington, his brother, Viceroy of India Richard Wellesley, and Sir Eyre Coote, commander in chief of the army in India and conqueror of the bogey of the British, Hyder Ali. There were distinguished aesthetes and collectors, like the flamboyant Frederick Augustus Hervey, Earl of Bristol and Bishop of Derry, whose taste, wealth and eccentricities are commemorated in two of the houses he built: Downhill in northern county Derry and Ickworth in England's Suffolk. Both were on the same plan, with a rotunda at the centre and every room on the edge of it possessing one curved wall, hard for design and the fitting of furniture. Downhill contained the works of old masters collected by him on his continental tours (his fame there led to the naming of a chain of luxury Bristol hotels). In the acres outside he had 200,000 trees planted, and built on the cliff top a round classical temple lined with books, to which he would repair alone at night. (Some mornings he would check the flour he had scattered on the floor of the servants' quarters to see who was visiting whose bedroom.)

For some reason the Anglo-Irish produced prolific inventors. There were polymaths like the amiable Richard Lovell Edgeworth of Longford, who invented a perfectly usable telegraph system for speeding the results of horse-races on their way, a wheel for a man to walk inside and thereby double his speed, a carriage moved by sails, an umbrella for haystacks, a semaphore, a velocipede, a road surface, a central-heating system and a prefabricated church spire. There were philosophers like the eminent Bishop Berkeley of Cloyne, who showed that there was no means of knowing St Paul's Cathedral existed unless you were looking at it. There were brewers like Arthur Guinness, inventor of what it was then deemed politic to market as "black Protestant porter". There were beauties like the Gunning sisters, who attributed the alabaster fineness of their skin — it was said that red wine could be seen coursing down their throats — to a peaty brown stream in which, as girls, they had washed themselves each day. Maria seems to have been a dumb blonde before her time, committing once the climactic Irishism of telling King George II that the sight she would most like to see was a coronation.

There were, of course, the writers. The climate that had bred the native storytellers — men ranked second only to kings in the eyes of the Celts — was well able to mould writers out of English stock. Once bred, though, an Irish paradox arose: they would not stay. Irish writers live anywhere but Ireland. The impulse to self-exile of those who draw their earliest impressions and inspiration from Ireland is documented as far back as the days of the missionary saints, and comes into our own era with James Joyce, Samuel Beckett and a dozen other contemporaries. It is the damp, say some; the drink, say others. Once it was the want and penury, another time the censorship.

Whatever it is and was, it was true of the the 18th century. Swift settled for Ireland only when his political prospects in England were dashed. Berkeley retired to a pleasant living and study of the universal benefits to be had from tar water after years in Europe, and years more in Rhode Island, where he pursued the aim of "converting the savage Americans to Christianity". Edmund Burke needed the Westminster parliament, the governors of a growing empire, intellects like Dr Johnson's, the buzz of a great European capital. Even so, he took Irishness with him, drank shockingly, and lived at Beaconsfield in a house whose dirt, dishevelment, and incompetent servants strongly reminded guests of his native land. Oliver Goldsmith and Richard Brinsley Sheridan spent few but their early boyhood years in Ireland, and having moved to Britain never went back. Yet each was a paragon of Irishness: Goldsmith kind, raggedly good-natured, improvidently giving his last shilling to a beggar, with a fund of knowledge and wit within him and a marvellous power of conservation; Sheridan the urbane, polished wag, dropping diamonds of wit about him in the drawing rooms of London and Bath; both adding classic comedy to the nation's theatrical repertoire. Indeed Goldsmith's *She Stoops to Conquer* and Sheridan's *School for Scandal*, *The Critic* and *The Rivals* are probably the only plays in a span of 150 years which still feature regularly in the repertoire. Amputate them, and the works of those late Irish dramatists Wilde and Shaw, and Britain's body theatrical is left a sorry cripple.

The Stirrings of Independence

It was small wonder, amid this excellence, the architectural magnificence, the pomp and ceremony, the intellectual energy and the constant glittering backdrop of Irish dialogue, that the ruling class of Ireland grew increasingly assured of its capacity to take over the complete management of the country, remaining loyal to the king in London but without obligation to his English government. This government they perceived as oppressive and discriminating, stifling Irish trade with its restrictions on manufacture and export. Moreover, Ireland had contributed well during the Seven Years War, which ended in 1763, and felt entitled to the reward of responsibility. More to the point, during the American War of Independence, the fear of invasion by France or Spain led to the raising of a force of volunteers capable not only of defending the realm but perhaps, with a judicious show of force, of winning rights, too. Self-government was demanded. The Earl Bishop of Derry seemed to imagine that he would be made king. He was disappointed, but Anglo-Irish Ireland was not. In 1782, the ancient Poynings' Law, which since Tudor times had made the Irish parliament subject not only to the king but to the English parliament too, was finally revoked, and Ireland became mistress of her own destiny. There was much celebration of the Irish nation coming into its own, though it was in fact an entirely Protestant affair.

The Protestants however were prepared to share some of their good fortune. The conciliatory Whig Henry Grattan achieved the repeal of most of the penal laws against Catholics, who were finally granted the vote in 1793. The main remaining planks of discrimination were the exclusion of Catholics from high offices of state, the bench and, above all, from parliament. At this stage, various events conspired to thwart them for another generation.

Maria Edgeworth (1767-1849), herself the daughter of an Anglo-Irish landowner, described the fecklessness, greed and absenteeism of some members of her own class in a series of novels of considerable literary merit.

Events in France following the first outbreak of revolution — the descent from idealism to barbarity, from claiming democratic rights to the guillotining of the king, queen, and as many as possible of the aristocrats — filled English and Irish alike, and particularly those with power, influence and most to lose, with horror and fear. Revolution was planned in Ireland, the government's spies were well aware of that. If northern Europe was polarising between the conservatism of Britain and the zealous radicalism of France, it was more than likely France would support Ireland's malcontents. Seeing no alternative, the government tightened its controls and dropped further reforms. In turn, a society called the United Irishmen laid plans for a national rising to tie in with a projected French invasion. The society was built on the noblest principles, and its leaders are among the most beloved in the national pantheon. Far from being sectarian, most of them, with Catholic emancipation among their most hallowed aims, were Protestant.

The verve and virtues of Wolfe Tone, the faith and fervour of Lord Edward FitzGerald (descended from those same Kildare FitzGeralds who had led a late Norman resistance to the Tudors), and the crazed courage of Robert Emmet have been enough to preserve their memories, for every Irishman can say or sing a ballad or two which tells of their bright hopes and the manner of their deaths, but they were not enough to change history. Tone's goodness and reasonableness shine from the pages of his journals. His role was to persuade the French to send a naval expedition — and after its failure, another — to assist a general Irish rising. The first fleet, in 1796, was hopelessly scattered by storms. The second was trapped and captured by the English. Tone, sentenced to hang, cut his throat with a penknife in gaol.

Lord Edward FitzGerald was a dashing officer and aristocrat, loved by all who knew him, married to a French beauty in a union of mutual devotion, whose irrepressible honesty forced him to throw in his lot with the revolutionary United Irishmen. They planned to revolt in 1798. Days before, thanks to the informers who had infiltrated the movement, the British authorities were able to swoop on a meeting of the leaders in Dublin. FitzGerald escaped and spent several weeks on the run. He was finally taken after an exchange of shots, one of which wounded him. He died in prison a few days later.

The third of these romantic heroes was so roundly beaten by fortune as to seem, at times, ridiculous. His rising came in 1803, two years after the union with England which had tipped the scales of power irrevocably in English favour. The rising he led, decked in a dandy uniform derived from French revolutionary wear, was muddled, ineffectual and smudged by the murderous tactics of some of its followers. He had for some time been secretly engaged to Sarah Curran, daughter of the leading radical advocate of the day. After the fiasco of his action, Emmet hid for a while, but was soon taken, tried and hanged. His speech from the dock — "When my country takes her place among the nations of the earth, then and not till then let my epitaph be written. . ." — placed him in a dignified position among the martyrs for Irish freedom, Curran though, learning of him daughter's liaison, forced her out of his home, and though she married within two years, she was dead within five, adding a degree of romance to a chaotic episode.

None of these individuals was able to take part in the rising which occurred in 1798. It was a wild and uncoordinated affair, most of its action confined to the southeast corner of the country. The Irish dependence, for want of money and arms, on the use of pikes led to engagements of great clumsiness and gore. Priests participated effectually on the Irish side: a signal example of the broad divide between parish priests and bishops, who generally allowed themselves to remain within the law and safety. Long after the main actions, with most fervour spent, a French naval force arrived off Mayo in the country's north-west. Though they marched far into the country, and on the way declared a local squire, John Moore, "first president of the republic of Connaught", they were eventually captured and conveyed by canal to Dublin, their band playing the *Marseillaise* on deck as they went.

The English prime minister, William Pitt, and most of his colleagues had by now decided that the Irish experiment with home rule had run long enough. It would be a constant threat to English security. He therefore proposed a union of the two parliaments, with the Irish contributing a hundred or so members of parliament to Westminster. The issue raised passionate feelings for and against, but Pitt was promising full Catholic emancipation to follow. Even so, it required bribery on an unprecedented scale, as well as the creation of dozens of peers and a certain amount of discreet intimidation, to persuade the Irish parliament to vote itself out of existence. The United Kingdom of Great Britain and Ireland was born on 1 January, 1801, and was to last for 120 years. Pitt's side of the bargain however was not fulfilled. It was not his fault; he wanted Catholic emancipation mainly because deprived Catholics were always likely to conspire with hostile foreigners and endanger the peace. It was King George III who refused emancipation on the perfectly valid grounds that it went against his coronation oaths.

Famine, Renaissance, Rebellion

The Deadly Blight

It was *Phytophthora infestans* which during the 1840s initiated a more radical and lasting change in Ireland than anything since the Anglo-Norman conquest. Population statistics tell the story more dispassionately than anything else. In 1800, at the time of the Union, there were about five million people living in the country. Twenty years later the figure had shot up to nearly seven million. The rise continued. By 1841 there were over eight million inhabitants, and by 1845 probably eight and a half. At this point Ireland's population made up about a third of the total of the British Isles. Ireland was one of the most densely peopled countries in Europe. Dublin was the kingdom's second largest city, yielding place only to London.

Within five years the population dropped by more than two million. Where there had been four people there were now three. The fall continued slowly but steadily until, by the end of the century, there were under four and a half million, and by 1961 only four and a quarter, half the 1845 figure. After rising in the prosperous 1960s and 1970s, more recently it has wavered up and down, but not enough to make much difference to the population contour of the last two centuries: a doubling over the first fifty years, a halving over the remainder.

The initial rise is variously explained. Factors which had kept numbers in check throughout history — disease, infant mortality, plague, famine, war — had been to some extent contained and controlled. People were marrying earlier. Ireland was getting richer. But the wealth was precarious, at least among certain sections of society. Though Ireland grew enough grain to feed the whole country, much of it was exported to England. The peasantry for the most part lived on potatoes, which were easy and cheap to grow and provided much more nutrition in a given small space than graincrops. Potatoes were required to feed livestock too: about a third of the national crop went to pigs. This dependence on a single root crop for the sustenance of so many people and beasts

76. The sport of kings has a fairly universal appeal in Ireland. The country has earned a wonderful repuation for breeding horses, and has exported some of the world's best known and fastest. It is said that a dealer can travel to England, buy a horse, bring it to Ireland, and on the strength of that provenance charge comfortably more than he paid for it.

77. The Irish have always been pioneers in racing matters. They are said to have invented steeplechasing and show-jumping, and they had betting shops thirty-five years before the English. Races keep bookies wholly concentrated on the question of odds, till the race begins and nothing can alter providence's edicts.

78. For some, betting is almost a science. They study form and compare results and scan each horse as it is led round the enclosure. For others it is a pin-point on a list of runners. For most it is somewhere in between the two. There is little to say which method is most reliable.

79. *If instinctive understanding of a horse's potential could be measured, it would certainly be found that there is more at an Irish meeting than among a similar crowd in any other country. For country people, horses are still a part of every-day living, and children ride bareback on ponies from early years.*

80. *A happy looking bookie suggests that favourites have not been winning. But then, bookies are careful to give nothing away in their expressions. Their speed of mind and action is phenomenal. Within seconds of the announcement of a photo-finish, say, or a stewards' inquiry, they have written up new odds for the outcome.*

81 and 82. You could cut the excitement with a knife. Upon this repetitive ritual depends the livelihood of thousands, the hopes and worries of hundreds of thousands, and the substantial fortunes of a lucky few. Radios all over Ireland (and tomorrow's morning newspapers) will be dispensing the wen of each race to betting-shop and home. And all of it is owed to the horse's love of a flat-out run.

81

82

83 and 84. For all its democratic appeal, racing can bring out what smacks of the ancien régime: *people whose clothes are of fine lawns and linens, tailored by experts, whose accents marry Oxford with the brogue, but who, being in fact Irish, know all about horses. The vestiges of the old social season linger on in Ireland, and races and the Dublin Horse Show rank high among them.*

85. 'A good jumper, is it?' said some Irish wit; 'and don't we have to inform the Air Traffic Control before we can let him out?' With the hills of country Kerry as a backdrop, the colourful cavalcade of a Tralee steplechase thunders round the course.

86. The newspapers give the runners, and sales would slump if they ceased to do so. The soigné elegance of the members' enclosure is quickly forgotten outside. The lady's bag probably contains a good flask of strong tea and some sandwiches and cakes.

87. Visitors always comment on the attractiveness of Irish children Their little faces often seem to speak both of innocence and suffering, and give the impression that there is nothing more that could surprise them.

88. Bare walls seem irresistible temptations to young artists these days, and in the North much of such painting is making a political point: for or against King Billy and Britain. This at Portlaw, county Waterford, is charmingly different, with its horses (including the hunting man on his mount round the corner), carriage, blacksmith's and assorted characters.

89. Ireland had its first betting shop in 1926. England had to wait thirty-five years before getting hers. They are now part of the scene in every small town, offering at least the dream of wealth and escape.

90. A sweet colleen in her Sunday best.

89

90

91 and 92. In Ireland, except in the bigger ranges of mountains, you are never very far from either a house or a horse. Grazing horses are part of every landscape. The Connemora pony, however, is more restricted in range, found mostly in the level lakeland of west Galway, where the Twelve Bens or Pins of Connemara rise like mountain fortresses from the plain. This is, beyond doubt, one of the most dramatically beautiful districts of Ireland.

93. Girl and horse seem to be enjoying a joke. Or has the horse said something rather risqué? Or is it confiding in her the news that over three thousand people in Ireland own bloodstock, and that these animals produce nearly half the number of foals born in the two countries of Ireland and the United Kingdom.

was dangerous. The peril began to show in the autumn of 1845, when the fungus *Phytophthora*, a well-known potato blight which had already done some damage to the English crop, was seen to be spreading in certain parts of Ireland. This was nothing new. It had recurred at irregular intervals of several years, and although it turned potatoes black, mushy and noxious, its depradations had always been limited. This year it went further. By October it had destroyed a fifth of the total crop. Not the least effect in the areas it attacked was the destruction of the seed potatoes which would have provided the following year's harvest.

Moreover, in the stricken regions, there were no potatoes to feed pigs with. Grain was used instead, or the pigs were slaughtered before their time. People were forced to eat grain too, with the consequence that grain exports were greatly reduced. So, of course, were farmers' incomes. Then, in the following year, the blight did what it had never been known to do before: it destroyed the whole potato crop. In spite of some emergency measures introduced by the government, and the tireless work of philanthropists, among whom Quakers were prominent, there was no way of averting tragedy. The blight was present for four seasons. During that period, something like a million Irish people died of starvation or disease, and more than a million sailed away to other countries, mainly America.

People were more to blame than nature. Throughout the famine period, Ireland produced more than enough to feed everybody, but landlords who were in a position to do so still exported large quantities of grain, though it sometimes required troops of soldiers to keep famished mobs from plundering it. Landlords did well in other ways. Death and emigration rid many estates of accumulated encumbrances of people and debt, making profit possible for the first time in years. Authorities naturally allied themselves with the owners of land, and insisted for instance that tenants forced by starvation and penury to move from a land-holding into a workhouse — their only chance of survival — should renounce their rights to the land before they were admitted. The London government introduced a mixed bag of measures. Some helped the poor. Others gave landlords the powers to evict tenants on trivial technicalities. Eviction often enough was followed, or indeed brought about, by the flattening of the peasants' cottage or cabin by police or hirelings armed with crowbars.

Nor could those who embarked for a passage to America be confident their sufferings were over. Some would never reach the far side of the ocean: "coffin ship" was the current term for old and overcrowded vessels quite unfit for the voyage. Those who arrived in Canada or America faced continued poverty, disease, cold winters and debt in the land of their adoption. Nevertheless, they helped each other, helped open up the unknown parts of the continent, and relished their freedom from English governments and landlords. They were followed over the years by more emigrants: the total by the end of the century was around four million, Within their intact Irish communities, the old grievances were kept alive and nourished right up to the present day. The rancour of the American Irish towards the British is usually sharper than that of the Irish in Ireland.

There was another side to the picture, and certain arguments which were often overlooked. Many landlords had been made desperate by the proliferation and congestion of peasant families on their land, living in and on ever smaller patches as sons divided their dead father's portion. In Ireland, unlike other countries where industries were growing fast, the increased population was clogging the countryside, not the towns. Disaster loomed anyway, from blight or cholera or some other epidemic, and only a disaster sooner could avert the inevitability of a disaster later. The landlords saw the Irish as boorish and idle (for growing potatoes needs next to no work), content to live and breed in a squalor they did nothing to change, accepting relief funds and using them to buy weapons for crime and banditry. Moreover, there were some Anglo-Irish families that laboured unremittingly to save those they felt responsible for. Some spent all they had on food for their starving tenants, only to find that other peasants came in from near and far to take advantage of their generosity. Such families died out or sank into obscurity as a result of their sacrifices and have had few spokesmen since. Others who had given much were accused of "souperism": doling out subsistence quantities of soup only to those who agreed to forsake Catholicism and become Protestants.

Charges, counter-charges, and the changing verdicts of scholars, who often unearth fresh evidence, have little relevance in the face of the resentment which grew out of the anguish and suffering of the Irish during those years. Passion overrides pretext, justification, and palliative. However much valour and self-sacrifice there may have been among certain of the governing class, it is the pitiless horror of the period which has lived, and in one way or another, directly or indirectly, coloured the attitude of everyone who has lived in Ireland ever since. The famine was a watershed. Before it, the faint possibility existed that the country could have progressed gradually to some inner equilibrium, in which the interests of Catholic and Protestant, northerner and southerner, landlord and tenant, might perhaps have been reconciled. After it, division, separation and continued hostility were inevitable. A true tragedy, in which guilt was unevenly distributed over the scene, had become a myth as enduring as those of Finn and Cuchulain, in which guilt rested exclusively on one side, and innocence and virtue exclusively on the other.

Gaelic Decline and Celtic Revival

Besides people, an ancient abstraction, the Gaelic language, went to the graves with the famine dead or was left behind to moulder by those who emigrated. English was the language of America. But English was also the language of England, where the 19th century saw a rapid accumulation of Irish people in such cities as Glasgow and Liverpool. Indeed, those who could judge the direction of things had long before seen that English was the key to life's more tangible rewards, while Gaelic was a barrier. For two centuries and more those Irish who resolved to raise themselves from their poverty and escape their smoky cabins had abandoned their language, adopted English, and anglicised their names. They did this in a variety of ways. They dropped the O or Mac which at one time preceded almost all Irish names; they translated names with actual meaning, so that for instance Mac an Ghabhann, meaning son of the smith, which was sometimes anglicised into MacGown or Gown, more frequently became Smith. And they smoothed and rationalised the spelling, picking the nearest approximation to the Gaelic sound: O Liathain, for instance, becoming Lehane pronounced Lehaan.

Daniel O'Connell, whose canny politicking and formidable mass meetings (attracting up to 40,000 people, and always peaceful) had finally secured Catholic emancipation — the removal of all but some negligible restrictions on Roman Catholics (they are still barred from becoming kings or queens) — had no wish to preserve the Irish tongue, though he could speak it himself. Swift, champion of the Irish people, had nevertheless proposed the abolition of their language, in order to "civilise the most barbarous among them". To find the Irish taking pride in Irish, it is necessary to go back to Tudor times, when Gaelic culture still had heart and bottom, and an O'Neill chieftain could exclaim that it did not stand with his honour "to writhe his mouth in clattering English". By the time the famine had devastated the country, the Irish language was in its death throes.

It is another of the paradoxes which punctuate Irish history that the death of the Irish language gave a new impetus to a number of movements and aspirations which

J. M. Synge. Courtesy of Bord Fáilte

John Millington Synge (1871-1909), the most gifted playwright of the Celtic Revival and Abbey Theatre, a master of "Gaelic English".

James Joyce (1882-1941), a central figure of 20th-century English literature, turned his back on the Celtic Twilight, leaving his native Dublin for good in 1904.

had Irishness at their core. The century which saw England slowly lose her grip on Ireland (home rule, if not full independence, became a near certainty before 1900) also saw the English language oust the Irish once and for all. Not that that brought the Irish and the Anglo-Irish closer together. The words they used were broadly the same, but the things they said and the way they thought were markedly distinct. The distinction is most apparent in the variety of visions for the future of Ireland which the different sects nourished. These visions, sown over the grave of the Ireland that had been destroyed by the famine, quickly became ideals — goals to be striven for. They were the blue-prints for the new Ireland, and as such they fashioned the new Ireland, some with more success than others.

For the Anglo-Irish, Ireland remained the dressing-up box it always had been, a place where reality impinged far less than in England. Estates became greatly reduced as the century wore on and governments granted the demands of militant Irish politicians. Rents naturally decreased, and with them incomes, but there seemed always enough to employ many more servants than was possible in industrial Britain, to keep horses, to hunt and entertain, to send children to boarding schools and universities in England (though Ireland now offered suitable cheaper alternatives), to be florid and eccentric, and quite often rather drunk, to omit to repair the roof when money was short and, instead, catch the drips of rain; and generally to cultivate a reputation of amiable oddity very much at variance with the prudent pragmatism of the English. Within this picture the Irish were expected to play their parts, doffing caps but not afraid of some cheeky banter, being picturesquely inebriated, late and muddle-headed, grooming horses, telling colourful tales, dancing jigs, and doing all the work around house and garden with broad toothy grins on their russet Celtic faces.

Those Anglo-Irish who fitted into this category — stage Anglo-Irish they might be called — were present in strength and conspicuous, and they have come down to us in the novels of Somerville and Ross, written around the turn of the century. One of the novels. *The Big House of Inver*, chronicles a century of decline in the fortunes of such a family. Prodigal spending and degenerate blood leads to the marriage of the eldest son into the agent's family. As time goes by, possession of the Inver estate passes to the agent's own heirs. Servant becomes master; master, not servant, but a rare and prized ornament to be shown off to friends. The process of conqueror succumbing to climate, drink, and native blandishment is the same one which afflicted the earlier Norman settlers in Ireland, and so exasperated the English authorities. It was not the only way members of the ruling class were drawn to Irishness. A much more alert and deliberate movement, whose leaders were almost entirely Anglo-Irish, was for the first time probing and studying the ancient culture which they had for so long lived among and ignored.

Other countries — Hungary, Italy, Germany — were doing the same thing, scouring their past for indexes of identity and the bricks of nationality. In Ireland the movement spanned the visual and literary arts. From the 1840s, societies were being founded for the purpose of resurrecting old Gaelic lore, studying early Celtic design, and printing texts and tales from ancient manuscripts. The discovery, in 1850, of the so-called Tara brooch, an 8th-century ornament of silver gilt set with glass and amber and decorated with delicate filigree birds, snakes, other animals, scrolls and braid, led to the serious commercial exploitation of Celtic themes. Silverwork and book illustration revived old, breathlessly detailed designs; and they were followed by furniture, buildings, carpets, wallpaper. Meanwhile, the literary researchers were unearthing rare delights: a huge body of myth that scarcely any European heritage, bar the Greek, could rival.

In 1880, one of these scholars, Standish O'Grady, completed publication of a bulky *History of Ireland: Heroic Period*. This brought much of the work of the previous forty years to the eyes of the public in a free retelling of ancient tales. The exploits of

Queen Maeve, Cuchulain and Finn McCool, of Dermot and Grania, the Court of the Red Branch knights and the swans of Lir, resurrected from cellars, vaults and attics, roused wonder and delight and a new pride in Celtic culture in the minds of readers. O'Grady — the Irishness of his name conceals a wholly Ascendancy background, his father being both a Protestant clergyman and titled — allowed his own dreams for Ireland to colour the telling of these tales. The aura of romantic courtliness he imposed on the stories was designed to do more than divert and entertain the reading public. It was intended to rouse the sense of responsibility of his class, and to stir them to take the lead in a Celtic renaissance that would unite the country. His success was limited. Most of the Anglo-Irish found that daily life left little time for cultural pursuits, least of all a Celtic restoration. Their vision of the future was as a continuation of the present, their own kind holding the reins of government without the violence and threats of violence which punctuated their lives, and at least retaining the decreased estates the Land Acts had left them.

Among one small group, however, the spark of O'Grady's narration was fanned into flame, and the great Anglo-Irish dream for the future of the country came into being. As a vision it turned out, in fact, to be short-lived and ineffectual. Yet the literary revival of the 1890s, and the associated ripples of literary distinction which floated out from Ireland during the first quarter of the present century were among the most extraodinary phenomena ever to have emanated from this puzzling and unpredictable country. It had nothing to do with Oscar Wilde, whose plays were nevertheless filling London theatres shortly before this decade, or with George Bernard Shaw, whose prolific output of wit and comedy kept audiences delighted for the next half century. The one was entertaining England in the tradition of Sheridan, with wit and epigram and very little to stir deep feelings; the other, Shaw, was entertaining but also preaching the gospel of Fabian socialism, as he would continue to do, in puckish, mischievous style, for half the 20th century. The champions of the revival had less commercial success than these two, and much less interest in it. Their movement was more of a crusade. Almost all were Protestant and Anglo-Irish, though there were Catholics among them. It does not seem to have worried them that those of less privileged, Catholic-Irish backgrounds might resent their appropriation of the native culture. When the realisation came, it struck painfully.

Yeats, Synge and the Abbey Theatre

Lady Gregory was the widow of a diplomat since whose death she she had cylced round the villages near her house in Galway collecting on paper the folk-tales the people could still recite from memory. She filled books with them, and wrote plays in "Kiltartanese", the English spoken by these Irish whose first language was Gaelic, and named from a local village. In 1898, she met the poet W.B. Yeats, a dozen years younger than herself. With others they planned the Irish Literary Theatre, which opened with a play of his in 1899. Among those who joined them were the novelist George Moore and the young playwright J.M. Synge. The assembled talent, of writers, actors and directors, was formidable. With the help of English patronage, they opened what Yeats called "a small, dingy and impecunious theatre" in Abbey Street in 1904. Within a few years the Abbey was one of the world's most famous theatres.

If the world was appreciative, the Irish by and large were not. Most had strict ideas about what constituted propriety on the stage. They could be touchy, over-alert to suggestions of vulgarity and blasphemy. Yeats first play, *Countess Cathleen*, provoked catcalls and abuse, but worse was to follow. The most dazzling wordsmith of the Abbey was Synge, whom Yeats had discovered in Paris and urged to move to the Aran Islands with the injunction: "Express a life that has never found expression." Synge's finest play, *The Playboy of the Western World*, staged in 1907, we have met before. Synge knitted the humour of the plot with a sparkle and beauty of language — again using the charm and freshness of Gaelic forms in English — which few could match. Despite all this, the audience was outraged. The amoral attitude of Synge's country lasses was taken as a slight on the piety of Irish womanhood. There were frowns at the frivolous treatment of murder. The dreadful word "shift" was used in the play. The response was a riot.

For all their genius and industry, the promoters of the Abbey were not clever in their attempts to alert the Irish nation to the need for an intellectual rebirth, a riddance of fossil attitudes, to match the political freedom they sought. Yeats's poetry and the honesty that shines out of his prose and verse will ring down the ages, but his attitudes could be silly, and his postures and dress — the Byronic neckerchief and dangling quiff of hair — risible. He plunged into spiritualism in any form and was undoubtedly fooled by some charlatans; he could surprise hosts by rising in the night to invoke the moon and see wild and beautiful visions. His head was not always in the clouds. He had endless earthy squabbles with Moore (who could himself be insufferable: "I came," he announced messianically, "to give Ireland back her language," which sounded odd from one who spoke no Gaelic) and discussed with all his friends Moore's irritating claims to a long record of sexual conquest. But the nature of his dream for Ireland limited the number of those prepared to assist him in achieving it. It was vague, visionary, and rather adolescent. He would attempt to unite theosophy and other mystical, cabbalistic forms with Celtic druidism (about which almost nothing was known), and designated a ruined castle on an island in the middle of Lough Key as a Castle of Heroes, where those promoting the new Celtic rebirth would return from time to time to charge the batteries of inspiration through contact with the divine.

By 1912 the movement was over. Philistine derision of the Abbey productions had killed it. Synge was dead, Moore back in England, Yeats disillusioned. The last straw was Dublin's refusal to allow the millionaire Sir Hugh Lane to finance the building of an art gallery in Dublin and to fill it with his collection, particularly rich in Impressionists. The building was to span the River Liffey in the heart of Dublin. Lutyens had drawn designs, but Dublin was generally of the opinion that home-grown architects and artists were just as good as English or French.

Abbey plays were lampooned by their enemies for the romantic and sentimental view they took of the Irish lives they portrayed. They were given facetious marks for the presence or lack of what was mischievously called "peasant quality". Behind these charges lay a confident certainty that Yeats and his cronies failed to get to the heart of Ireland because they were moulded of English clays. Like others, Yeats had been to school in England when his volatile father moved the family there for two years. The literature and history he knew were English. Ireland was a foster parent, for whom his affection seemed preposterous.

Land Reform and Boycott

While plans were being laid for the Celtic Revival, during the 1890s, two much less romantic ideals were being pursued by hard and pragmatic men. The traditional rulers of Ireland were going to learn, within a few short decades, that the granting of political concessions — the removal of the penal laws, and the more positive legislation to transfer ownership of land from Anglo-Irish landlords to tenants — would not arouse gratitude in the beneficiaries. Such steps never did. Between 1870, when the prime minster, Gladstone, introduced the first land act to divide up the great estates among those who worked them, and 1909, when the last such act was passed, the number of Irish householders in possession of some land rose from three to sixty per cent, and the redistribution of land had gone as far as it might reasonably be expected to go. Yet within a few years of that last act, revolution broke out.

The Irish had had their fill of colonial condescension. Their own organisations were going to be uncompromisingly hostile to the Anglo-Irish, pushing their own cause without wish for compromise or conciliation. Where the Anglo-Irish did help them — and plenty did — it had to be at the cost of renouncing their background. The harshness of this attitude pervaded most strictly Irish organisations. The hundred or so Irish Members of Parliament, ranked until his undeserved disgrace in 1890 behind Charles Stewart Parnell, sold their block vote only for legislation to help the Irish, and when they withheld it, nearly brought the Westminster government to its knees.

At home, the Parnellites urged all their followers to cut off all contact with any landlord or agent who went ahead with unjust evictions, "as if he were a leper of old". The first target of this campaign was Lord Erne's agent. Suddenly he found himself unable to hire men to work, or to buy or sell farm produce, while his wife was refused service in local shops. Other landlords provided him with labour, and 7000 police and troops were brought in to keep the peace. But in the end he had to move out. At least he has an immortal memorial in the language: his surname was Boycott. Meanwhile, the Catholic priests, flexing their muscles in the newly won status assured them when the Church of Ireland was disestablished, became tough and unyielding. The teaching order of the Christian Brothers disseminated a history which stressed English villainies, and even a century later, in the 1950s, the Archbishop of Dublin, Dr McQuaid, would be forbidding Catholics to attend Trinity College, though the college had long since rescinded its own ban on Catholics and was anxious to make amends.

In the world at large, it was Yeats and his circle who made the greater impression. Their aspirations have coloured vividly the general picture of Irish aspiration. Ireland itself did little more than pay them lip-service.

Thomas Moore (1779-1852), poet and songwriter, whose "Irish Melodies", based on traditional airs, have retained their popularity down to the present day.

The GAA and Gaelic League

The movement which put down successful roots from end to end of the country was the Gaelic Athletic Association, founded in 1884, which was dedicated to the promotion of traditional Irish games. Such an aim could be expected to dovetail neatly with the artistic and literary revival, but the founders of the GAA were determined that it should not. No less than fostering Celtic games — hurling, Gaelic football, camogie and handball — their aim was to exile the traditional English games of cricket, soccer and rugby. It called these the "foreign games", and it forbade its members to play or attend them — a ban which lasted up to the 1960s. The intention behind such rules was evident and, on its own terms, sensible: to make breathing space for games which were being pushed into oblivion by introduced English sports. But from the beginning the GAA attracted other more political factions, most importantly the revolutionary Fenian movement, which was able to use the organisation's concern with the most innocent of pastimes as a front for its more sinister and seditious activities.

Parnell himself could be said to be the victim of the inflexible forces of nationalism. In the 1880s, he seemed the most important man in Ireland, regarded by many as an unofficial king. He had ridden several attempts to discredit him, including the printing of some scrurrilous forgeries in *The Times*. Then, in 1890, he was named as correspondent in a divorce case. He had lived with the woman, Kitty O'Shea, for years,

and pleaded that his public and private lives should be distinct. But, along with other bodies, the Irish Catholic hierarchy condemned him. He struggled to retain the leadership for a year, but the strain killed him in 1891.

In 1893, another organisation came into being, founded on the wish to conserve and restore the native language. The president of the Gaelic League was Douglas Hyde, the son of a Church of Ireland parson, who had learned Gaelic and written poetry in both languages. His other passion, on which he wrote a famous lecture, was "The Nececessity for de-Anglicising Ireland", in which he advocated the resuscitation of everything Gaelic, from language to dances and songs, with the consequent banishment of English practices. At first the enmity to the Anglo-Saxon was less evident than the desire to revive the Gaelic corpse, and for a while Yeats, Hyde and their respective colleagues respected each others' ambitions. But Yeats, in spite of his naive credulity in some other matters, never thought the Irish language could entirely replace the English, and still less that its literature could oust the brimming legacy of England's. Hyde and his fellows did. Their campaign to spread Irish touched a nostalgic nerve in the minds of thousands of their countrymen. In a few years there were well over five hundred branches of the League all over the country, Irish had to be taught in schools, and proficiency in it became a condition for entry to the national university. A wit warned that this measure would make most Irish illiterate in two languages. Predictably, nationalist agitators found their way to the top of the League, and in 1915 Hyde himself resigned as president for that reason. By that time Patrick Pearse, whom many regard as the founding martyr of Irish independence, had described the league as "the most revolutionary influence that has ever come into Ireland", to be mentioned in the same breath as openly militant revolutionary organisations.

One of the more curious aspects of the League was the debate that went on within its ranks about the provision of an Irish literature for the Irish to read when they renounced English. Various solutions were proposed, but all had to acknowledge that there was simply not, as yet anyway, enough Irish to fill the gap. Certain Irish authors — the popular poet Tom Moore was one — were therefore allowed to figure on reading programmes as temporary stopgaps. In time, contemporary and future authors would, it was assumed, supply all needs. Of course it is in the nature of fervent idealists, planning their Utopias, to think along such lines, blind to their absurdities, blind also to the implications of political control over literature and the easy descent from this to general censorship. In the event, when the new state of Ireland emerged from painful nativity, the censorship it imposed was immoderate, banning some of the work of almost every Irish author of note (and so depriving readers of a peculiarly rich and vibrant literature, and living authors of their livelihood). Moreover, the plan to replace English with the Irish language would be regarded by most people today as a costly failure. In many schools it became the medium for teaching not only literature but also subjects like history and mathematics. Yet there was never the slightest chance of English being displaced. Not English, but education itself was the casualty; and within months of leaving school most Irish people had consigned the language of their forefathers to the same dusty mental archive as logarithms. It mattered not at all that the constitution named Irish as the country's first language.

To the visitor today, the visible remnants of this campaign are few, often rather quaint, sometimes irritating. Gaelic is not an easy tongue, and to complicate matters, several distinct regional dialects of it are maintained. Its spelling, though simplified from time to time, has nothing but its letters in common with English. On street names, signposts and buses it can, unless the English equivalent is displayed (which is not always the case), be utterly baffling. Fortunately the Irish name — say, An Nuaimh — seldom appears on a signpost without the English version — Navan — being shown too. And in the areas known as the Gaeltacht, in which Gaelic is the first language of some 40,000 people, natural courtesy would instantly cause a conversation to switch to English if someone ignorant of Gaelic were present. Many people, too, have opted for the Irish spelling of their names, and not a few speak Irish among themselves in the privacy of their homes, including middle-class homes in the smarter suburbs of Dublin and Limerick. For the fondness for the idea of a national language understandably persists, as does admiration of the unique quality of old literature written in Irish. Yet many would say that the famine and its aftermath saw Irish to a grave in which it should not have been disturbed. And many would add that the Irish are quite different enough from everyone else without having to adopt a language nobody outside the country understands.

Militant Organisations

Yeats's Celtic Revival held stage for a while, left an indelible mark on European civilisation, but — too dreamy and cerebral — scarcely touched the bulk of the population. It was the unsmiling, uncompromising face of nationalism which defined the direction Ireland took during the 20th century. There was the Gaelic League and the GAA. Linked to them, more or less formally, were the various armed factions, not all pursuing the same dream but willing to overlook their differences to achieve independence. (It was characteristic of these years that the idea of home rule — a partial independence, fostered by moderates headed by Anglo-Irishmen — gave place to insistence on cutting all but the most nominal ties with Britain.) James Connolly's Citizens' Army was socialist; the Irish Republican Brotherhood enjoyed strong support from capitalist America. The Irish Volunteers came into existence initially as a response to open arming by the militant Orange interests in Ulster. All these were preparing to fight, parading and drilling in uniforms and carrying firearms in the streets of Dublin. Other organisations contributed moral, financial and technical assistance: the political party Sinn Fein (pronounced "chin fane" and meaning "we ourselves" to signify the national self-reliance it envisaged), and the various nationalist women's and children's associations.

It was an Irish organisation wholly out of sympathy with all of these which provided the main trigger for armed rising. By 1912 home rule had been promised by the Westminster government, though there were constitutional hurdles to jump. Early the following year the Ulster Unionists, fiercely opposed to any Irish breakaway, and utterly determined that the Protestant North would remain part of Britain, paradoxically established an army, the Ulster Volunteer Force, to resist the decisions of the parliament they intended should continue to govern them. The 19th century had not brought them an inch nearer to the Catholic population. The famine had far less impact on the northeast than elsewhere in Ireland, mainly because it was heavily industrialised. The Presbyterian settlers had remained completely immune to those Irish characteristics which transformed the earliest Norman settlers and made the Anglo-Irish distinct from the English. They retained the virtues they had brought with them from Scotland: thrift, punctilio, cleanliness, dogged strength. (Their stolid integrity has led many otherwise Catholic firms to employ Protestants as accountants.) They and the English Protestants had built up industry and commerce and created the city of Belfast, which began the 19th century with a population of 20,000 and ended it with more than ten times that number. Their drive and prosperity, and the admiration they aroused in the English, caused the government to tolerate the wholly illegal means they were now using to thwart the granting of independence. They smuggled illicit arms into the country, and they paraded and demonstrated all over the two islands. The government turned a blind eye (though it busily arrested the much less provocative suffragettes of the day). The

Welcome in **FITZPATRICK'S** *Second Hand* **SHO**

OPENING HOURS
Mon. To Fri. 9.30am - 5.30pm
Sat. 10am - 5.00pm

94. *Considerable ingenuity goes into the decoration of the exteriors of shops and other buildings, frequently with much bold use of colour. Often enough the lettering is handsome. This shopowner has added an effect of his own: what amounts to a small museum of rural life displayed on the upper wall.*

95. *County Clare has always been the home of the best folk music in Ireland, and the small seaside village of Doolin has in recent years become a sort of musical Mecca. McGanns is one of the three bars in the village that put on live music in the evenings.*

96. The Crown Liquor Saloon in Great Victoria Street, Belfast, is the only pub owned by the National Trust. Built in 1895, it is still lit by gas. - All the fittings and contents have a rich period flavour, as can be seen in the decorations on the window.

97. Barrels of whiskey at the Bushmills Distillery on the coast of north Antrim. The process was invented by an Irishman. and later taken to Scotland (where slightly different methods of heating are now used, and where the drink is spelt without the 'e' normally used for Irish). Among other kinds, Bushmills makes a rare Irish malt.

MUSIC
IRISh COFFEE
SANDWICHES
SOUP
FRESH SALMON
SANDWICHES
IRISh COFFEE

98. At the Blue Loo Bar in Glengarriff, county Cork, a witty decorator has shown on the outside wall the fate that alwaits any full glass of beer or stout. The Irish coffee offered consists of coffee, whiskey and cream. It is, of course, not an Irish tradition at all: the peasants of old did not go in for such indulgence.

99. Not so many years ago, a woman in a bar would have been thought a brazen creature. Tourism has inured even the most chauvinistic Irishmen to the invasion.

100. Musicians are traditional, but some of the instruments have gone through some modifications in recent years.

101

102

101. *Relaxing time outside the Blue Loo Bar in Glengarriff. The man on the left appears to be amassing a store of beer, while two of his companions could do with refills. There also appears to be a fashion hereabouts for combing a man's hair forward.*

102. *The Irish face slips naturally into a smile.*

103. *The slogan that has lasted three generations: 'Guinness is good for you'. Before the days of the advertising agencies, Guinness kept ahead of its rivals by offering prizes for advertising ideas. Now, in spite of stiff competition and some seamy associations of the name with dubious financial dealings, it still manages to lead the field.*

105

104. *The colour of the barman's hair and his wedding ring add to the golden glow given off by the brass fittings and the colour of beers in the Crown Liquor Saloon in Belfast.*

105. *The eyes of barman and customer are on the same attraction, probably a television set. At a quarter to four in the afternoon, perhaps the conversation on offer is not as good as the box.*

106. *Not that conversation completely dries up at any time of day.*

106

107. Tourism has forced all kinds of changes on the Irish bar. This pub at Bunratty stacks bottles of mead on its shelves. Perhaps tourists imagine the drink goes back in an unbroken tradition to the medieval feasts they are led to believe took place in the castle next door.

108. A lovely lass drinks the truly traditional beverage. Arthur Guinnes, founder of the firm, began brewing at Leixlip in 1756.

109

109. *The Rusty Mackerel pub at Teelin, county Donegal, set on Teelin Bay and on a wild mountainous coast. As often, a* trompe l'oeil *artist has been busy on the right.*

110

110. *To many an Irishman of the older generation, this is the best moment of the day: work done, washed and brushed, a comfortable seat, friends on their way, and a good froth-capped pint to get outside.*

111. *Heavy partitions divide the space in many pubs, giving the effect of a train dining-car. The Irish like the feeling of intimacy produced by such arrangements. The extreme form is the so-called snug; these are virtually tiny rooms, which in the past might have their own fireplaces, where the privacy is almost total.*

112. *Cider barrels feature among the empties outside this handsome inn. The most successful newcomer in the towns, though, is wine. Its consumption shows every sign of increasing as Ireland follows the middle-class trends of neighbouring Britain.*

114

113. Combining the businesses of bar and grocery is very common in Ireland. Less common, but known, are the combination of bar and cycle repair shop in Cork, and bar and bespoke tailor in Clare.

114 and 115. A feature of working in a pub is that your customers, in most cases, get happier the longer they stay, while the risk of complaint diminishes. The people shown here seem entirely satisfied with the value they got for their money.

116. Hurricane Higgins is only the most famous of thousands of Irish snooker players, many of whom acquired their first enthusiasm for the game in pubs. This player is special: Roger Bush, thirteenth generation owner of the Billiard Room at Narrow Water Castle, county Down.

outbreak of European war in 1914 became a new government excuse for delaying home rule, and although thousands of Irish volunteered to fight against the Germans (more perhaps for regular pay than out of a desire to defend king and country), the more determined nationalists decided that an armed rising.

Easter 1916

The Easter Rising of 1916 was by no means a triumph of administration and logistics. It was hampered by contradictory orders given by the leaders, one going so far as to call the thing off in a newspaper announcement. Nor did it enjoy the blessing of the majority, or even a substantial minority, of the population. Throughout its short duration, scarcely more than 2000 insurgents took part. It was extraordinarily Irish. Easter Monday was a particularly fine day, and vast numbers of Dubliners had left the city for the horse-races and seaside, or picnics in the hills to the south. Any who happened to be in O'Connell Street just before noon might have seen about 150 armed men in familiar green uniforms rush into the classical portico of the massively domed General Post Office. A few minutes later, one of these men begain to address the passing public: ". . . Ireland through us summons her children to her flag and strikes for her freedom. . ." Nobody took much notice. Similar scenes were being enacted in other parts of Dublin: the Castle, St Stephen's Green, the courthouse, and half a dozen more.

At Stephen's Green a man driving a horse and cart was irritated by the erection of barricades across the paths. He remonstrated. Young insurgents shouted abuse, and one gave him a count of four to drive away. He stayed put, was shot in the head, and killed. Suddenly, an Easter Monday masquerade had become a bloody revolution. But it was days before it seemed to be. There were brushes and skirmishes here and there, but mostly the rebels did the only thing they could do, which was to stay put and wait for the British to assemble a vast armament of retribution. As the English troops began to march in, some of them were astonished to find themselves under fire from snipers. They had assumed they were in friendly France and addressed the locals with smiling "bon-jewers" and "parlay-voos". But the ships behind them had powerful artillery on board, and their incendiary shells were soon blasting the scattered rebel quarters. O'Connell Street was virtually destroyed and whole blocks of houses were on fire. The casualty rate rose to something like 450 in all, with thousands more wounded. The respectable citizens of Dublin were understandably outraged. As individual rebels were arrested and led away, bystanders threw rotten fruit at them and shouted "Shoot them! Bayonet them!" and worse. It had all been a dismal failure.

Within three weeks it became a resounding success, at least on its own terms. With the powers given them by martial law, the British sentenced ninety of the leading insurgents to death. The penalty, by shooting, was carried out on only fifteen. It might not seem an unduly harsh response for the time, given the number of innocents whose death the rising had caused, and the feeling of treachery that it had come in the middle of a war. Nevertheless, law-abiding Irish were horrified by the executions — not least by the final shooting of James Connolly who, injured in the fighting, had to be brought in an ambulance to the prison yard and tied seated in a chair to be able to face the firing squad. The grisly work of those days transformed men who had seemed like gangsters and lunatics into martyrs. The blood sacrifice envisaged by Patrick Pearse and his comrades when they picked the central Christian festival for their action had come about. People who had been sympathetic to the British authorities now prayed for full independence, and it was only six years before that was granted, at least to the twenty-six counties which professed to want it. 1916 was both nothing much and everything: a brief chaotic interlude and the founding of the modern Irish state.

Division and Integration

Birth of the Irish Free State

Though it achieved a somersault of Irish opinion, 1916 drew no concession from the British. Nor did the next nationalist triumph, when the Sinn Fein party won three quarters of the Irish seats in the 1918 general election. Several of the successful candidates were, in fact, in prison for sedition, and none took up a place in the Westminster parliament. Instead they set up an Irish government (*Dail* — pronounced "daul" — *Eireann*), and began making their own laws as if there were no other authority in the land. Britain, emerging from world war, and strongly sympathetic to the Protestant loyalists of Ulster, took the firm repressive line. From April 1919 to July 1921, an ugly guerrilla war of mounting bitterness blighted Irish life. On the strongly disputed grounds that the force was bigoted, partial and against them, the Dail passed a resolution ostracising all members of the police force, the Royal Irish Constabulary. The Boycott campaign was being revived. In return, both Sinn Fein and the Dail were declared illegal. Thus the only effective legislature on the one hand and the only body capable of maintaining law and order on the other, became constitutional cripples. There followed attacks on police stations, individual soldiers and policemen. Again the government came up with an answer. It recruited from the teeming population of British ex-servicemen an ill-trained and not too fastidious force whose brief was to meet violence with violence. In March 1920, the Black and Tans, as they were called, began to arrive.

The months that followed brought out viciousness in both sides, and left indelible memories of wanton, brutish behaviour, even more reprehensible perhaps in the official forces of the imperial power than in a guerrilla force without, as yet, any legal standing. (Yet the dangers of taking on that touchy imperial power now its authority was ebbing must have been obvious. Only a few years before, in the market square of Amriksa in India, British troops had, on a major's orders, massacred four hundred peacefully assembled townspeople.) The callous, bullying behaviour of both sides is not in question. Those on the nationalist side, previously known as the Volunteers, had by now given themselves a more formal name: the Irish Republican Army, or IRA. A name to last.

In 1920, in the middle of this campaign, the counties of the North accepted the home rule which, until the Easter Rising had made nationalists more ambitious, would have suited a large majority in the South, too. It was indeed offered to the South. The proposal involved a parliament for the North, and another for the twenty-six counties, as well as substantial Irish representation in Westminster. Sinn Fein rejected it, and the North accepted. From then on there was to be no acceptable squaring of the interests of the two.

The fighting continued until the middle of 1921, when it was clear that no dent had been made in the nationalists' resolve, and that the people of Britain and America were appalled at the mounting ferocity. The death the previous autumn of Terence MacSwiney, Mayor of Cork, whose arrest for sedition had led to his going on a hunger strike which lasted seventy-four days before he died, had deeply impressed the public of both countries. (Cork had suffered inordinately from the Black and Tans.) By late 1921, negotiations were in train between the Westminster government and Sinn Fein. Early the following year, the Irish Free State came into being.

The names of the southern and northern divisions of Ireland have always been problematic, at least until the South left the Commonwealth and became a full republic. *Eire* is simply one of the Gaelic names for Ireland, and was incorrectly used for the South

"The Emerald Isle and Fenian's Home". An American Fenian map with portraits of distinguished Irishmen.

alone. The northernmost tip of Ireland is in the "South". The ancient province of Ulster included three counties which are not part of the northern state. "Free State" pleased nobody, but at least it had a Gaelic equivalent, *Saorstat*, important in a country whose first language was intended to be Gaelic. The English prime minister, Lloyd George, teased the Irish delegation with the fact that the Gaelic civilisation they so cherished lacked a word for the political system they aspired to, a republic.

De Valera and the Republic

For the time being the treaty granting independence stipulated continued membership of the British Empire and the gesture essential to it: an oath of allegiance to the British Crown, to be taken by all members of the Dail. Although an Irish general election of 1922 approved this, certain leaders of Sinn Fein were adamant in resisting the imposition of such an oath. These, under the leadership of Eamon De Valera, split off from the main party, took to arms, and initiated a gruesome year-long civil war. Only a handful of years before it had seemed as if a second Irish golden age was imminent: a new birth, freedom from an army of occupation after almost 750 years, the realisation of small-nation ideals after a century in which the world had seemed dominated by avaricious empires. Now Irishman was killing Irishman, blowing up some of the finest buildings in the country, setting fire to houses, ambushing, sniping, assassinating. Eamon De Valera's Republicans lost the war — though neither side could be said to have gained by it — but he himself soon began to show that sombre dignity, slightly obfusc argument and air of pious dedication to the well-being of independent Ireland which kept him close to the summit of Irish politics for almost forty years.

His party, Fianna Fail, swept into power in 1932. He endeared himself to many Irish by bravely refusing to yield land annuities to Britain. These annuities were repayments of loans made by the British government years before to enable tenants to buy the land they had occupied. De Valera's stand was based on Britain's annulment of such debts for the Northern Irish. Britain retaliated with punitive import duties. Ireland, which could less afford to, did the same. The so-called economic war broke out and continued to 1938, when a single lump sum payment settled the annuity question. De Valera's David had boldly struck the English Goliath.

Not all the Irish were content. De Valera's dream was, in his own words, of "a frugal, good-living and Gaelic New Jerusalem". It was to be a very Roman Catholic New Jerusalem, Catholicism being given special status in the country by the new constitution of 1937. It tried to impose stringent moral guidance, but of course there are only some areas where that can work. Censorship was one. The board already set up to impose it had started with little opposition, banning the more lurid and sleazy English pornography, whose purveyors were always hoping for Irish sales. Now it took to a Grundy-like posture, and was soon outlawing undoubted literary excellence. Hardly an Irish, let alone a foreign author escaped without one or more works being proscribed, with consequent loss of income. Lists of the authors whose work was treated in this way have often been printed: Joyce, Graham Greene, Somerset Maugham, Hemingway, Thomas Wolfe, Naomi Jacob, Eric Linklater, H.E. Bates, and so on. Meanwhile, fine artists, sculptors commissioned to do work for public display, would have it turned down if the nude human form were represented, however chastely (though a nearly naked Christ on the cross was always welcome). Till the 1950s, jazz was forbidden on state radio, and any remotely favourable reference to contraception or abortion in literature was expressly forbidden. Films, too, already laundered by Hollywood's own vetters (who allowed a man on a bed with a woman only if fully dressed and with at least one foot on the floor), were heavily and absurdly cut.

All of this would have been less hypocritical had it not been for the new use, as well as the familiar ones, to which the big neighbour Britain — now a foreign country — could be put. Travel between the two islands remained without any restriction. No passports were required either way; indeed, Irish citizens resident in Britain have always had the right to vote in British elections as well. Throughout the 20th century, innumerable Irish have settled in England to earn better money than they could at home, sending part of it back to their families, and in many cases returning home when they felt they had earned enough or qualified for a pension. Now, however, a lot of Irish found it convenient to go to England for those things Mother Ireland forbade. They went to get divorced, to buy contraceptives (a legal anomaly allowed suitcases full of them to be brought into Ireland, but none to be sold), to have abortions, to live as man and wife when unmarried, to read uncensored newspapers, to get radio and television stations that never broke into token periods of Gaelic, and to breathe more cosmopolitan, less sanctimonious air. It is impossible, of course, to say how many Irish took advantage of any of these possibilities, and how many simply went to England to earn a bigger wage. But England undoubtedly provided a safety valve for a country which was taking itself very seriously.

The War and Its Aftermath

The Second World War did not help matters. It was probably inevitable that De Valera should choose neutrality in 1939. England, not Germany, seemed to many Irish to be the country with jackboots on. All the same, sitting on the sidelines isolated the Free State, except for those 50,000 of her young men who volunteered for service in the British armed forces. The North was involved, Belfast being badly blitzed in 1941 (and, in fact, receiving prompt help from the Dublin fire brigades). The South shared neither the suffering of the war years nor the joy and reconstructionist fervour of peace. The war was officially and distantly referred to as "the Emergency". Fastidious in his neutrality, Mr De Valera even called on the German ambassador to offer condolences on the Fuehrer's death. When the war came to an end in Europe, the news could not — again for reasons of her neutrality — be published immediately in Ireland. The editor of the *Irish Times*, the most serious and at the same time least nationalistic Irish newspaper, simply set all printed matter on the front page in the shape of a huge "V".

Most of the Irish rejoiced at the allied victory, but this could not prevent a profound feeling of estrangement and a gloomy inertia taking hold of Ireland in the years that followed. She was alone. Catholicism had not come well out of the war. Ireland's politicians were short of imagination. Most of them were the same men who had fought in Dublin in 1916, or against the Black and Tans four years later and against each other in 1922. Many of these were to be joined and in time succeeded by their sons. Nepotism appeared to thrive, and it seemed as if the stirring days of independence had been preserved in moth-balls which threatened to deaden all change and innovation. Prominent politicians were where they were not on account of political or economic knowledge and expertise, but because of fighting or firebrand talents long since disused. A mustiness pervaded the political scene, from which thousands of young people departed as emigrants.

It did not greatly help matters that the revival of Gaelic was still central to Fianna Fail's programme, and to a lesser extent that of the other main party, Fine Gael, although it was perfectly clear to many that the average citizen, while praising the Gaelic ideal and happy to have his children reach basic proficiency in the language, neither could nor wanted to give it the same attention he gave to English, the language of newspapers, books, magazines, radio, films and the medium which would soon surpass all others in its power to influence, television.

But there were men waiting in the wings to grasp the economy and squeeze it into better shape. The idea of the common market of Europe, which would so greatly benefit the economy and raise the morale of Ireland, was just around the corner. An era which would scatter new bungalows across the land and breed generations of smart executives, upward mobility, affluence, blocks of steel and glass and concrete to replace the mouldering brick and stone of inner cities — that era was near at hand. It was as if a spring would shortly be activated that would hurtle Ireland forward half a century or more to set it alongside its fellow Europeans. But before any of these things happened, there were things about Ireland which, despite her fustian, dilatory, postwar mood, made her most markedly and uniquely valuable.

A Land Left Behind

It was a generation or two ago. Ireland was not only behind the times, it seemed to see no point in getting in front of them. Not in material terms, at least. There was in Ireland the space and beauty that only an inconceivable increase in population could obscure. Cars rolled along the uncluttered lanes, and the main roads, though no motorways, were adequate and seldom crowded. Railways were pleasant too, the rolling stock cosy and old-fashioned, and converting rather late to diesel from steam. "Dear, dirty Dublin", a 19th-century author had summed up the city she lived in, and "dear" and "dirty" were adjectives which could still apply to all towns of the Republic — less so Northern Ireland — and to many of the villages. People's clothes were patched, and a lot of things were done up by safety pins. Telephone operators, being local, listened in to conversations, and might tell callers the person they wanted was not in and where he or she might be found. If money was short, time was plentiful. If someone, friend or stranger, began a conversation with an Irishman engaged in some occupation, his activity would, unless lives depended on it, cease; and until the talk was over he would betray no urge to return to it. An awful lot of tea and sweet biscuits were consumed. On the national scale, the country seemed to have been mercifully spared the industrial revolution. And it lived up to its Christianity, sending astonishing numbers of missionaries all over the world; and ready to serve to under the unromantic aegis of the United Nations Organisation.

Friendliness seemed to go along with contentment. Unshaven faces broke easily into natural, toothless smiles and laughter. Old people in particular made remarks that seemed philosophical, based on long thought and experience. Outside certain areas of the bigger towns, there was very little crime: country people did not lock their doors, and often could not, for want of keys. Manners were good and natural. Burying the dead involved prayers and tears, followed by drink, food, stories, song and dance. One curiosity was that, for good or ill, Ireland seemed very unsexy. The Irish colleen was famous for her lovely looks and animated ways, but, though she might flirt, she was not a slouch or tramp, resisted allure and glamour in the Hollywood style, and was often noted for hard work and piety. Some Irish men seemed indifferent to the charms of the other sex, and certainly in this period they married far later in life than the men in other countries — at an average age of nearly forty.

There were attempts to explain this. One theory was that drink had far too strong a hold on the Irish male. The woman he felt safest with was his loving mother. Otherwise, security was to be found only in the pub, fortified by a few pints. Romance was a painful interlude, brought on by the divine injunction to be fruitful and multiply, and he did this only when he had some savings under the mattress, and perhaps when his mother was dead. His wife was much younger than he, bafflingly bright and demanding. Not long after the honeymoon, he avoided her when possible, staying late at the pub as he had before marriage. For company his young wife had to be content with her children. The man in her life was her son. She indulged him and guarded him jealously. He grew up feeling safe with his loving mother or in the pub, fortified by a few pints. . . So the cycle continued.

Doubtless there was some truth in this, yet it was a very partial truth. Domestic secrets are not as easy to obtain in Ireland as in America, and nothing said about them can be altogether relied on. The rate of childbirth — the only real proof apart from invasion of the bedroom — indicated that Irish sex happened, and happened reasonably often. It was made less of than elsewhere, but it was easy to argue that elsewhere it was made too much of — in easily available pornography, girlie advertisements, erotic clothes. Inhibition knotted people up and sometimes made them rather weird, but the most liberal societies had weird members too. Though repressive monkish teaching doubtless tangled the psyches of many, Irish reserve about sex could be seen to be old-fashioned, nicely balanced, and rather charming.

In the Republic, the Catholic Church was very much in evidence. Towns could seem medieval from the ratio of clergy, monks and nuns, of all orders and seemingly all nations, to be encountered while walking along the streets. The bell for mass cleared a country village entirely. People on foot or on buses crossed themselves when they passed a church or a shrine or a grotto to the Virgin Mary or the place where a patriot had been killed. In Galway, impoverished peasants were contributing their mites to the building of the massive cathedral which now dominates the skyline. Houses abandoned by the departing gentry were bought by the church to be used as monasteries, convents or seminaries; and a new priest seemed to come off the production line every minute or so. Thousands of people, some hardly more than babies, some very old indeed, flocked to the great Irish pilgrimages, to climb Croagh Patrick in July, and endure joyfully the rigours of penitence on an island in Lough Derg in Donegal, in which St Patrick once found the gateway to purgatory; and to the great foreign pilgrimages of Lourdes and Loreto. Thousands of Irish men and women served abroad, all over the world, as missionaries, relieving pain, teaching, and as they saw it, saving souls.

Nowhere in western Europe or North America was quite like this, and everyone who came to Ireland from one of these countries remarked on its many unfashionable and unpriceable advantages. Many returned to it year after year. (The exception was a certain kind of American of Irish stock. He was capable of being critical, telling the Irish how this or that would be done, so much more efficiently, at home; and that if the decision were his, he would have, say, an office block here and a warehouse there, and work would start at six instead of ten and. . . bob's your uncle, it couldn't lose. In this there spoke, perhaps, the son wishing to impress his mother on his return from travels.)

People generally thought Ireland had something special, something spiritual almost, and that the Irish, in ignoring so many of the preoccupations of other races, were retaining a sane balance. Some of these people began to settle: the English, as they always had done, but French and Germans as well. A lot of English settled to peaceful craft pursuits in county Cork and are still there. Germans, in particular, seemed to think that this laughing, singing people, as removed as it was possible to be from the *Sturm und Drang* of their own racial ethic, held life's secrets. They bought estates all over the place, but it is hard to become something you are not. Some Germans irritated their new neighbours by putting wire fences where patchy hawthorn had served before, loudly barring trespass. Not all of them stayed, but many did, and gradually assimilated. In time, the Japanese arrived. One, a factory manager, told a television interviewer that he felt Japanese no longer: he was now, he said, completely "Ilish".

Things were different, and some things were uncannily similar, in the North. The North was a province of the United Kingdom which had come into being to enshrine a Protestant majority. Initial plans to include all Ulster had been dropped because three of Ulster's nine counties had Catholic majorities, and there would have been a danger, given the higher Catholic birth-rate, that the province would develop an overall Catholic majority able, among other things, to vote itself out of the United Kingdom. The North was earnest and industrious, and Harland and Wolff of Belfast was the largest ship-builder in the world. The province was also very religious, with all the sects being hyper-active in a partly competitive spirit. The Presbyterians' passion that they should never be subject to papism in any way had not abated. They believed in the scarlet woman of Rome, stained with sin and superstition. And they hated her followers. To limit Catholic influence in the province, they had from the beginning arranged constituencies and other boundaries to the detriment of Catholics. For instance, on polling day the residents of a Catholic street would have to walk through an exclusively Protestant area to reach the polling station, something they might deem unwise. Local authorities looked after their own in matters of housing and other benefits. It was clear that no election could ever change things. Only some kind of protest might.

The issue, though related to it, was not exactly the same as the question of relations between North and South. In the middle 1960s, the prime ministers of both parts of Ireland made history by meetings at which they smiled and joked with each other in front of cameras, and discussed ways of ending the hostility between the two states. Such fraternising, particularly from the Northern point of view, was till then unthinkable, and it offended diehard Protestants. The Republic's constitution, they always remembered, stipulated that the whole of Ireland was by rights one country (and an officially Catholic one) even if violence as a means of restoring the unity had been renounced. There was no more point in their respective leaders meeting than there would have been in talks between Christ and Satan to settle their differences. Agreement was simply not a possibility.

In the Republic, the 1937 constitution's affirmations did not quite reflect the reality of politics. The old divide still existed, between those who accepted the compromises contained in the 1921 treaty and those who had gone to war to repudiate them. There was still an Irish Republican Army, recruited and trained in both parts of the island, and ready to conduct guerrilla warfare to bring the North under Dublin's control. It chose the civil rights campaign as a pretext for starting the battle again. The Protestant or Orange elements of the North had their own fighting units, which, like those of the IRA, were outside the law. To minimise the violence, large numbers or British troops were stationed in the North. Police forces on both sides of the border were increased. They all clashed, in every conceivable combination, and horror succeeded horror. The uncomprising anti-Catholic stand taken by the Northern government (often known by the name of its parliament house, Stormont) led to its suspension, and direct rule from Westminster. But the two remaining governments, those of Westminster and Dublin, had their hands tied tightly. Dublin could never admit what was probably true, that it did not want the North; not at least with the other things it would have to cope with: terrorist organisations which would almost certainly bid for political power, the desperation of the Orangemen, the loss of the stabilising effect of Britain. And British politicians could never contemplate the abandonment of the North, or dealing with "terrorists" whom — despite frequent claims to the contrary — they were clearly unable to beat and who, often enough, were the only civil authority with any influence in the so-called urban ghettoes. As the 20th century entered its closing years, more than a

117. *The owner of the Augher Castle Hotel in county Tyrone takes his three hunting dogs on a wildfowling expedition.*

118. *The flimsy-seeming curragh or coracle has been used in the west of Ireland since prehistoric times. Traditionally made of skins and twigs, it was often used for the transport between island and mainland of full-grown cattle. This one is very futuristic: it has a motor attached.*

119. *A fisherman leans against a bollard and relaxes with a newspaper close to his nets.*

120. *A finely marked goat and a family of tourists stand in the foreground, while county Clare's Moher Cliffs taper away in the distance. These sheer striated cliffs, consisting of layers of sandstone topped by a bed of dark shale, stretch for about five miles, with views across to the Aran Islands.*

121

121. Ireland abounds in water. Sea, lake and river provide a dazzling plethora of fish of all kinds. Fishermen are not wanting, yet the proportion of humans to water precludes all possibility of crowding.

122 and 124. Joe Beattie, owner of the Augher Castle Hotel in county Tyrone, goes duck-shooting around the edges of his lake.

12

123. On the quiet waters of the lake outside Westport House in county Mayo, a number of young geese experiment, unsuccessfully, with the baffling procedures of taking off.

126

127

125. *At Kilsheelan, a small village in the south of county Tipperary, a signpost bristles with directional information, while a model woman leads her model donkey and milk-cart among the carefully tended flowerbeds. In her enthusiasm for the Common Market which served her so well at first, Ireland embraced the metric system. It will be noticed that while most of the figures refer to kilometres, the distance to the Rosminian Novitiate, like most people's spoken directions, is given in miles.*

126. *A real woman, real donkey and real milk cart, sheltering from the rain in Glenbeigh, county Kerry. Most milk churns have been abandoned in favour of the giant milk-tanker.*

127. *A farmer takes a ride in his donkey cart close to Dingle on the peninsula of the same name in county Kerry. Donkey numbers go down, but the west, in particular, finds plenty of uses for them.*

128. *Ireland dramatically displays the reasons for her alternative name, the Emerald Isle. The colour is achieved at a cost. In parts of the west in rains on average every other day throughout the year, and reaches a total of 120 inches. Even so, Irish rain tends to be what the Irish call soft: a gentle, vaporous affair, soon dried off by a good breeze.*

129. *The River Barrow meanders lazily through the luxurious verdure of county Carlow.*

130. *A horseback ride through the leafy lanes in autumn.*

131. *Birds flock in the evening over a sea inlet. Ireland is particularly rich in sea and estuary birds, for obvious reasons. Off the south-west coast are several islands occupied by huge colonies of gannets. Estuaries tend to ring with the plangent calls of curlews along with the pipings of oyster-catchers, dunlins, redshanks and sand-pipers.*

132

133

132. *Fog hangs low over the hills, and the shapes of the hawthouns on the left speaks of almost uninterrupted exposure to the prevailing wind — both indicators that the sea is close.*

133. *An old man dismounts on the slope, and his dog is pleased to relax the pace.*

134. *A typical rural scene offers a mountain (seldom more than 3000 feet in Ireland), a winding lane, a bungalow and a cottage or two, an untidy line of telegraph poles, and various shades from rich deep copper to pale green.*

135. *The parents and grandparents of the people occuping these houses on the west would have been well acquainted with hardship and hunger. They were lucky if they possessed a donkey cart, and the diminutive patches of grass between walls were unable to support much livestock. The Common Market subsidy, and the spread of the economic benefits of industry and tourism, have allowed the present inhabitants to build new houses or spruce up the old, always remembering room for their own cars and those of their guests.*

136

136. An exceptionally neat, rectangular arrangement of dry stone walls. Like other European countries, Ireland has been through a period in which the black-and-white Friesian cow outnumbered all others, and seemed set to extinguish them. Systematic breeding programmes have, however, brought back other varieties, which will restore a lost colour-richness to many rural scenes.

137. Sheep nibble the grass without soiling it; unlike cows, whose urine makes, collectively, large areas they would never eat.

138. A painted caravan like the travelling people, once called tinkers or gypsies, used to live in. This one is in county Wicklow. The firm which rents it out says Germans and Dutch are the most frequent hirers.

141

142

141 and 142. The pedestrian bridge over the Liffey in the middle of Dublin has been known as the Halfpenny Bridge since the days, earlier this century, when a toll was charged for crossing it. Its alternative name is the Metal Bridge, here floodlit to a lurid green.

143. O'Connel Street by night. This is the main thoroughfare of north Dublin, leading away from the central hub of the city, O'Connell Bridge. Lacking much architectural distinction, it contains a number of statues on its central islands, including those of O'Connel himself and Parnell. Nelson was there till 1966, on a high central column, but to most Irish this essentially English hero seemed very out of place. One night ne was blown away by dynamite, nobody discovered by whom.

144. The General Post Office on the west side of O'Connell Street holds a special place in the history of Irish nationalism. It was here, in 1916, that Patrick Pearse and others started their Easter rising, occupying the building with an inadequate troop of Volunteers. A week later the British, after initial uncertainty (and distracted by the European war) pounded the building with artillery, destroying much of the street as well. The execution of the ringleaders brought a wave of Irish sympathy which made independence inevitable.

145. Statues above the pediment of the Post Office, and one the lamps on a central island of O'Connell Street.

146. In Merrion Square, FitzWilliam Square, and a number of streets north and south of the Liffey, Dublin possesses some of the finest Georgian domestic architecture in what used to be the British Isles. Those who bought plots of land along these roads agreed to certain general points of design, but were left some freedom, which gives terraces like this an edge over more uniform housing of the period, as in Bath.

147

147. *The river Lee flows through the middle of Cork, and the city, unlike others in Ireland and Britain, does not ignore it or turn its back on it, but lines it, for much of its length, with handsome buildings. The wedding-cake steeple in the background, belonging to the church of Holy Trinity, was restored to dazzling splendour in 1982.*

148. *The Memorial Arch on the north-west corner of St Stephen's Green in Dublin commemorates those of the Dublin Fusilers who were killed in the Boer War: 212 names are engraved on the inner walls. Through the arch are the delightful landscaped pleasure gardens which were given to the city by a Guinness in 1880.*

149. *In 1769 a young English architect won a prize of £ 100 for his design for an Exchange building. He went on to design many more of Ireland's finest Georgian buildings. What was called the Royal Exchange was subsequently used as a barracks, a prison, and a corn exchange. Since 1852 it has been Dublin's City Hall.*

150

150. *Under an elegant lamp bracket outside Trinity, Dublin's chapel, a wedding party waits. The chapel was designed in the 1770s by Sir William Chambers, who was at the same time perfecting his plans for Somerset House in London.*

151. *Shops, shoppers and traffic pack into the winding high street, which like most others contains some nice architectural oddities, notably the terraced building half way along on the right with four heavy pediments on its first-floor windows.*

152. *The attention to details of design — the handsome lamp standards and elaborate door hinges picked out in red — make it the more astonishing that Ireland can allow so much of her old building heritage to fall into ruin. But more than appearance is in question here: to too many Irish, beautiful buildings still smack of the unacceptable rule of Westminster.*

153. *The name of the Rob Roy bar suggests a Scotch connection. Northern Ireland has many such. Western Scotland was originally colonised from Ireland — Argyll means 'eastern Gael' — and northern Ireland was in its turn, in the 17th century, colonised by Scottish Presbyterians.*

155. *An unusual brass door-knocker: the kind of detail in which the older buildings of Ireland abound.*

156. *Identical Victorian doorways, with fanlights of simple tongue pattern and elegant Ionic columns on each side, enclose doors that differ in colour, design and the positioning of brass letter-slits.*

157. *Some of Ireland's older doorways are sadly neglected, like the two in this picutre. Fanlights need complete reconstruction in both.*

158. *This doorway in Merrion Square is like most of its neighbours, very well maintained. Once residential (Oscar Wilde lived in the square as a boy), it now houses firms of solicitors, architects and others.*

159 and 160. Conformity is not the Irish way. The Irish cherish little differences and distinguishing details.

161. This doorway, on the face of it identical to number ten in the picture opposite, has in fact a dozen small differences.

160

161

162. The brass plaques on this pink door are reminiscent of the medals that jangle on a Ruritanian general's chest.

163. Brash kindergarten colours distinguish this doctor's doorway.

162

165. *The surge in tourism has caused whole vil-*
lages of holiday cottages to sprout in places
where, in the past, cottages went to rack and ruin
for want of occupiers.

166. *Among the features that distinguish North-*
ern Ireland from the Repubblic are the telephone
boxes: the red box is British, and has no Gaelic
lettering. In the Repubblic the boxes are blue and
white and have the Gaelic name — almost identi-
cal to the English — as well as the English.

167. *A sheep auction in progress at Maam Cross,*
a road junction in the shadow of the Maumturk
Mountains in Connemara.

168. *Connemara men carry on their quiet, con-*
spiratorial conversations, always inaudible to
bypassers, at Maam Cross.

169. A pretty sky puffs up behind a landscape of sheep, orchard trees, and neat fencing. Skies are one of the visual delights of Ireland. Except on sodden, foggy or overcast days (of which there are not a few), the prevailing south-west wind brings a constantly changing skyscape from its journey over the Atlantic.

170. *The gnarled and bony limbs of the western Irish landscape. There, mountains are always close and fields are spotted with boulders or hirsute with heather or reeds; and ruins are sprawled untidily among them.*

172

171. Most Midland lakes as well as all the main rivers contain trout, and a few conceal salmon. But salmon have to be tough and wily to survive. Apart from their migration to Greenland, they are netted at the entrances to their favourite Irish rivers and at stages upstream by men with ancient rights to do so.

172. Another picturesque sky looms up over the harbour and a riot of ox-eye daisies.

173. A quiet corner of the gardens of Birr Castle, county Offaly, home of the Earls of Rosse. The gardens are among the best in Ireland, with lake and river, terraces and parkland, covering about a hundred acres.

173

174. *A mountain stream gains width and depth as it reaches the peaty plateau below the steeper sloper. Such water tastes good, and is the basis of all good whiskyes.*

175. *Rain, mist and fog are, it is true, one of the conditions of Ireland. Visitors have pointed out what a blessing this is. If there were less precipitation and more reliable sun, the place would be quite overrun.*

176. A character in Synge's play The Playboy of the Western World *talks of two lovers 'gaming in a gap of sunshine'. Here is one, lighting the gold autumn grasses of the Wicklow mountains.*

177. In the rich and fertile flatlands of the centre and southern midlands mile upon mile of barley and wheat come to ripeness.

1

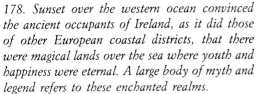

178

179

178. *Sunset over the western ocean convinced the ancient occupants of Ireland, as it did those of other European coastal districts, that there were magical lands over the sea where youth and happiness were eternal. A large body of myth and legend refers to these enchanted realms.*

179. *Along the north coast of Antrim, several castles are perched precariously over the sea, but none offer such a romantic outline as Dunluce here. A McDonnell stronghold till Elizabethan times, and scene of several sieges and other dramas, it was abandoned in the 17th century after part of the building and several servants fell away into the sea.*

180. *A shipwreck joins the hundreds of other lying under Slea Head and in the Blasket Sound at the western end of the Dingle peninsula in Kerry. Among them is at least one vessel from the Spanish Armanda. Having been repulsed from their invasion of England by storms and Francis Drake, the Spaniards sailed round the north of Scotland and down the west coast of Ireland to regain Spain, but lost innumerable vessels on the way.*

181. *Adare Manor in county Limerick, an example of the Tudor revival in the mid-19th century. It was till recently the home of the Quin family, Earls of Dunraven, who maintained a reputation for care and generosity towards their tentants, which so many others signally failed to achieve. It has recently been converted into a hotel.*

182/3. *"These are the clouds about the fallen sun, The majesty that shuts its burning eye".*
W.B. Yeats

184/5. *The tranquil beauty of Ireland's landscapes, the soothing greenness and rolling hills, have always inspired Celtic bards, whether at home or scattered around the globe.*

186. *The Japanese garden at Tully House near Kildare. The garden was created in 1906 by the great Japanese designer Eito, who made the Japanese garden at Powerscourt in the same year. Tully House is the seat of the prosperous government-owned horse-breeding establishment, the National Stud.*

187. *A glimpse of medieval beauty from the decorous comforts of the 19th century.*

189

188. A scene in Grafton Street, the centre of Dublin's higher quality shopping area, shows the perseverance of two tough Irish traditions. The world 'Debs' on the advertisement points to the survival, despite unpopularity, of an exclusive social stratum; while the boy rattles his box for the benefit of one of the most respected Catholic charities, the St Vincent de Paul Society.

189. The vine-leaf gates at Powerscourt, county Wicklow.

190. A winged statue and urns at Powerscourt, county Wicklow. The magnificent gardens have huge terraces, lakes, and arboretum, and a staggering view of the conical Sugar Loaf mountain in the distance. The house, a Wingfield property for most of its existence, was burned down in 1974 and most of its rare and valuable contents were destroyed. The shell still overlooks the gardens.

190

191. *Students of Trinity College, Dublin, take in a bit of commercial activity during the afternoon. This is in the so-called Parliament Square, just inside the main gate of the college. The pedimented building on the right is the Examination Hall, opposite the matching Chapel. The hundred foot high campanile straight ahead was built in 1853 on the supposed site of a medieval priory church.*

192

192. *Shoppers pause appreciatively by musicians playing traditional folk music, for which the Irish have an inexhaustible appetite. Instruments are not always as traditional as the music.*

193. Until it began to paint itself in bright colours, the village of Sneem on the Ring of Kerry ws unremarkable, except for the beauty by which it was surrounded. The daring use of colour, and a craft cooperative, have brought it fame and revenue.

194. More bold colouring and a catchy name attract the customers.

195. The Sahara look comes to the shop windows of the damp and sea-girt island.

194

195

196. *Nice and unusual colouring for a house with an antiques business in the village of Bally-moe, in east Galway.*

hundred years after the Liberal prime minister, Gladstone, had tried repeatedly and with immense foresight and courage to get home rule for the whole of Ireland, a fragmented Ireland could look ahead to nothing but violence and deadlock in the matter of boundaries.

Social Trends

All the same, these matters of state were not able to alter certain social trends to an extent, the whole of the western world was experiencing them, brought about as they were by sweeping technological advance, expanding markets, spread of education, the levelling out of class and income, improvement of communications. The differences between peoples were being ironed out. As long as hardly anyone in a western Irish village had a television set or a motor car, that village was thrown onto its own devices, which made it singular. It had its own character, and its inhabitants had very distinct characters too. It had a certain monotony, suffocating to many expansive young minds. The car threw open lines of connection. Relations moved from one place to another, then friends, then sports teams. Telephones augmented the process, though Ireland was slow to get a telephone to most homes. The greatest challenge to the insularity of villages and hamlets came from television, and that, even before it was in every home, was in many pubs. Homes along the east coast had only to raise their aerials twenty feet to receive several channels of British television.

Irish emigrants in the mid-19th century, a period of mass exodus to escape social and economic ills (painting by Erskine Nicol).

Early in the 1960s, an interviewer named Gay Byrme introduced a programme on *Telefis Eirean* called the *Late, Late Show* which has been running on Friday evenings ever since. It was a chat show, nothing unusual for television but unheard of for Ireland because the participants were invited to talk about anything. Reactionary priests, flower children, liberal schoolteachers, caning head-teachers, homosexuals of both sexes, people against and people in favour of abortion and contraception and feminism and capital punishment, whites and blacks, Protestants, Catholics, Jews, Muslims, and ever-available politicians all at one time or another came on to say their say, argue their corner against sometimes steely opposition, laugh, be laughed at, and often enough demonstrate to viewers who might never have believed it that they were perfectly reasonable people; not squint-eyed and dirty-faced, as Northern children are often taught the children of the other sect are, not necesarily perverts or bigots or anarchists or racialists or satanists. Whatever it did to underlying attitudes, it enabled people to think a little and say something about subjects which would have struck them dumb with disapproval or embarassment before. It was sophisticating.

Pope John's Ecumenical Council moved things in the same direction. Exclusivity was one victim. Latin, which had made Catholic services incomprehensible to outsiders, and to most members of the Church, was thrown out of the window. So was a lot of the more arcane ritual. Churches and services were shared with Protestants from time to time. The stuffier aspects of paternalism were being weeded out, and feminism would be quick to move into the vacated space.

Feminism, however, had a lot of resistance to overcome. Women had always had a respected place in Irish society: goddesses in pagan times seem to have been so important that some of them, when Christianity came, had to be smuggled into the new religion in a kind of disguise. There is good reason for thinking, for instance, that St Brigid or Bridget, the chief female saint in the Irish calendar, was the old goddess Brig metamorphosed. Such things are well attested elsewhere, and the fact that several centuries after her death a perpetual flame was kept in her honour indicates pagan connections. Mariolatry, the worship of the Virgin Mary, considered a serious heresy within the Catholic Church because Mary was not a part of the divine Trinity, has often been associated with Ireland for the same reason. The Irish like goddesses. Doubtless, Irish feelings on the matter helped bring about Vatican concessions, the most significant of which were acceptance of her own (as well as Christ's) immaculate conception, and of her bodily assumption into heaven.

Women played a part in the struggles for independence in the early part of the century, and the women's nationalist organisation *Cumann na mBan* was as uncompromising as De Valera over the Anglo-Irish treaty concessions. Maud Gonne, the woman Yeats loved without requital all his life, remained a famous fighter for women's rights, as well as Irish freedom, for all her nearly ninety years, publishing, founding women's clubs and leagues, and demonstrating (earning herself six months in gaol in 1918). Constance, Countess Markiewicz, another friend of Yeats's youth, went further. In 1916, commanding a contingent of rebels at St Stephen's Green, she gave her first order to kill, and was rewarded with the blood of a young English soldier.

But independent Ireland seemed for long very much a man's world. Women remained on pedestals, but pedestals from which they had easy access to the kitchen sink and the broom cupboard, thus according with the principles of Mr De Valera's frugal New Jerusalem. However, since articulacy has never been a male monopoly in Ireland, they were eloquent in staking their claim to the equality the 1970s and 1980s seemed to demand: and though their ratings for income and share of the job market are among the lowest in Europe, they improve faster than some.

Another change of recent years which chimes with the *zeitgeist* has been in the

attitude to the Gaelic language. It was another part of the old and somewhat impractical vision of the new Erin that everyone should be fluent in both languages and, if anything, marginally more so in Gaelic. Converted from vision to policy, Gaelic became a chore. Proficiency was necessary for jobs in the civil service, for teachers and, strictly speaking, for members of the Dail. There was genuine fondness for it, for its differences, for the way it symbolised a vanished heritage. But English was more than adequate for verbal communication in most countries in the world. Especially Britain. And even more specially, America.

America was moving in. It will never oust English influence because England is a few minutes' flight or a few hours' sailing away. Moreover, at any one time there are a million or so people of Irish birth living in Engalnd and earning wages, part of which will be remitted to Ireland. And the North, for good or ill, is a problem shared by both countries. But American influence is increasingly seen and felt in Ireland. There is, to start with, a common historical bond of resistance to imperialism. America was the first territory to fight its way out of the British Empire, and Ireland was the second. Both countries resist English formality and protocol. The garish, vulgar aspects of America, seen in shop-fronts, some clothes, some foods, some entertainments, are frequently duplicated in Ireland.

America is also deep in the Irish economy, investing in industry, opening and running factories that will give access to Europe, subsidising research and development in response to Irish expansion of higher education. It is present in all kinds of smaller local schemes, often because of family ties. Americans buy, live in, and so preserve some of the finest Anglo-Irish country houses and castles. Not long ago, a Philadelphia millionaire left the nation in his will a sumptuous baronial pile, Glenveagh Castle, in Donegal, together with thousands of acres of lake and mountain. American money largely finances the heroic Irish Georgian Society, which battles more successfully than any other body for the conservation of fine 18th-century architecture.

Poster to recruit southern volunteers for the
British Army in the First World War.

Into Europe

Since 1973, Ireland has found yet another orientation which will perhaps prove the most important of all. Although there was no serious alternative for Ireland once Britain had decided to join the European Common Market, it was this same market which offered some relief from excessive dependence on Britain. Membership promised a lot of financial support for farms — and Ireland's farmers made up a much more important chunk of the economy than those of most other countries; and further benefit from the Community's Regional and Social Fund. She made application to join, as Britain did, in 1961, and was, as Britain was, turned down. Twelve years later, after referendums in both countries had returned massive majorities in favour, both countries joined. A few years rendered Ireland the net beneficiary of hundreds of millions of pounds. But far more important was the voice she gained in international matters, the entry to a forum the like of which independent Ireland had never had a place in, the ability to influence European and even world events. It was a coming of age, half a century after the state's foundation. It offered also a hope that Europe would take the limelight off parochial matters like the differences between North and South. But the first couple of decades of membership did little to justify that.

During the campaigns which preceded the referendum, a poster appeared everywhere in Ireland. It showed a cabinet meeting, with twenty or so smartly suited men with well-brushed hair and urbane expressions sitting round a large polished table with the usual carafes of water, glasses and pads. To see how this could be part of a political campaign, a foreigner needed to read the caption. In so many words it said: Look, they are just like the British cabinet sitting round *their* polished table in their smart suits. Is this what we had a revolution and a civil war for? To ape our former masters? To become the same as them?

It had made a smart rhetorical point, but it did not go on to answer implied questions: How else should they be dressed? What should they sit on, and what should they put their pads and pencils on? They were not questions worth answering. It is true that certain romantic aristocrats of the 19th century, to show their solidarity with the Celtic cause, always wore the saffron kilts supposedly the garb of true Irishmen before English ways polluted the country. The politicians could have worn these. They could perhaps have sat on the massive flat stones that kings and princes of ancient Ireland were customarily crowned on. It would have seemed eccentric, but it would have been Celtic. And it certainly would have excluded them from office at the next election.

The real point of the poster was that it appealed to a rather vague nostalgia, common to most Irish people, for times gone by and tempting might-have-beens. The feeling of loss in there, and growing. The more the smartly suited politicians strut the world's stages, the more an Irish premier fulfils his turn as European president, the more American tycoons sign contracts over breakfast at Shannon stopovers, the more yuppies with brogues Ireland breeds, the more scope exists for such feeling. It is part of modern life to know and regret the disappearance of things we love, and to enjoy things we may not love so much but which we are not prepared to do without. We let go of clean streams, old woodlands, donkey carts, even the languages of small nations, in order that we may have money, business, commerce, profit, cars, air-conditioning and other means to desirable ends. This happens just as much in Ireland as in other countries. It would be unfair to ask otherwise.

Still, people will and do. Perhaps because the one thing almost everybody takes for granted about Ireland is that it will not do exactly the same as every other country. In that distant period when Ireland was perhaps most herself, what they call her golden age, scholarship and theology were being neglected all over Europe until the Irish came in small numbers here and there and restored the love of study and prayer and monastic disciplines. There are all kinds of possible reasons why the Irish should have been peculiarly fitted for this role, but the only thing of consequence is that they did it. Forty years ago, when the important historical truth about Ireland was that she was on her own, unloved, poor, and badly governed, everybody who visited the country from abroad remarked on the indescribable glories of land and charm of people.

"The Gael is not like other men. . ." Patrick Pearse's overblown speech comes back in such a context. We try to shun sentimentality, even though not only Pearse but Yeats himself succumbed to it. We try to stick to facts. Ireland is not her rulers, not the politicians, national and local, who lard the debating chambers with cliché and platitude, or cause to be erected, as the Dublin Corporation recently did, two big white ugly boxes of offices on the very site where the Norsemen placed the nucleus of the city — and overlooking and obscuring, for good measure, the medieval cathedral of Christ Church. Ireland is bigger than and beyond her politicians, as most countries are. She is certainly rather special. Science recently disclosed that Ireland is quite literally one of the four corners of the earth: four areas of several hundred square miles which are truly some 120 feet above the geodetic mean, and where the gravitational pull is proportionately greater than elsewhere. (The others are in the vicinity of Peru, Japan and South Africa). But there are more convincing, less whimsical arguments. Because a generation has turned its back on the countryside, it does not mean the countryside has disappeared. People building Moorish-arched bungalows are not, mercifully, pulling down older and better buildings to do so. There are still the ruins of monasteries, churches, ascetics' cells, and the amazing sense of spirituality that comes over the most hardened unbeliever at the remains of Ciaran's monastic schoool at Clonmacnoise or the fragments of St Fechin's Fore Abbey. Pilgrimages produce astonishing physical feats, sometimes by people who are plagued with paralysis or some other handicap. There are people who have never stayed a night away from home, more than content with the sunsets, foamy rocks and ever-changing colours of the mountains of their native west. Worship of the horse survives from the old days and shows no sign of diminishing, and a skin and wicker coracle with an outboard motor attached is only fractionally different from the old-fashioned one without. Irish bulls — the joke kind — are made in every town several dozen times a day. The stage Irishman is alive and well. Around the coasts, the curlew and oystercatcher pipe plaintively as they did when Queen Maeve ruled Connaught and Cuchulain saved Ulster from defeat. There is in short magic in abundance. A country so pervaded with the enchantment of the past may go any way but an ordinary, average way.

Landlords sometimes paid the price of ruthless exploitation.

The Irish Abroad

Rudyard Kipling tells of a man who visited a native house in Tibet and found that every child within it had flaming red hair. The owner did not know why. What he did know was that his own father, whom he hardly remembered, had owned a red coat and expected his sons to stand upright when he shouted the mysterious word "Shun!".He had owned an English gun, and instead of the usual Tibetan gods he worshipped a cross. The son had inherited cross-worship from him, and with it a hymn which, though he did not know its meaning, he would croon with his wife:

Dir hane mard-i-yemen dir
To weeree ala gee.

For a second it seemed to the visitor like mumbo-jumbo. But suddenly all was clear. The song's words were a simple corruption of those of a popular Irish revolutionary ballad:

They're hanging men and women too
For the wearing of the green.

The father had of course been a Redcoat, a soldier in the British army, who had married a native Tibetan woman, settled, and bequeathed red hair to his grandchildren. That made him probably Celtic, the song certainly Irish. He was one of uncountable numbers of his countrymen who had been whisked from their own land to strange and remote places by some centrifugal force. The Irish are among the most restless migrants in the world, and have been since they learned how to build skin-and-whicker coracles and sail away from their shores.

The earliest to leave their own land did so to grab that of others. In the 4th century they made raids on the west coast of Britain, looted goods and people, and planted many Irish colonies in Cornwall, Wales and Scotland. It was one of these piratic gangs which kidnapped the young Patrick who was destined in due time to convert to Christianity the country of his captivity.

This pugnacious buccanering seems to have come to an end more or less as the new religion took root in Ireland. From then on Ireland conquered no-one, nor tried to. Inhabitants left their country in large numbers either to help others become Christian or to find better conditions thant those they were accustomed to: to secure God's grace for themselves or for others.

It was the urge to proselytise which sent hundreds of Irish to Britain and the continent in the 6th and 7th centuries, and in diminishing numbers thereafter. Christianity had reached the Irish late — 432 is the date when the adult St Patrick is supposed to have arrived on his mission — but it pleased them so well that within a few decades they wanted to tell the world about it. This missionary movement, which led to the founding of numerous European monasteries and the improvement of the discipline and scholarship of many others, may also have been the reaction of a people too long cut off from the romanised, progressive world outside. They wanted to join in.

Curiously, the Irish have not generally made good explorers. There were a few. St Brendan, whose exploits were examined in chapter two, may even have discovered America before the Danes or Welsh did, but he was one of the exceptions. This is surprising, for all the other countries of the Atlantic seaboard — France, Spain, Portugal — sent out navigators who helped to open up the world. But then, after the Anglo-Norman conquest of 1170, Ireland was not her own country. The capital investment for risky expeditions of discovery came from London, and it followed naturally that the men who crewed them were mainly English.

Attempts by the English to control Ireland were stepped up in Tudor times. After any sort of rising, and sometimes on some feebler pretext, Irish families were dispossessed of land, and English planted in their place. Of the old inhabitants, some settled in the inhospitable west of the country, while many more fled to the continent, sometimes in the wake of defeated chieftains, who could not accept the imposition of English government, like the Earls of Tyrone and Tyrconnell, who led the doleful "Flight of the Earls" in 1607. During the remainder of the 17th century the policies of the Stuarts and those of Cromwell to Ireland showed no essential variance from each other or from those of their predecessors. All were bent on anglicising: on making the Irish renounce Rome and speak English. And failing that, on smashing all obstacles the Irish presented to their distributing and managing the land in the best interests of England. Again and again shiploads of Irish sailed away in defeat and despair to the continent. They served, some with great distinction, in the armies of France, Spain, Austria, Italy. The Irish regiment in the French army had the satisfaction of defeating the English at the battle of Fontenoy in 1745. Two generals of Irish extraction commanded the armies of Maria-Theresa of Austria in the late 18th century. During the same period Irish colleges were founded at all the great Catholic cities in Europe, to provide advanced education for Irishmen whose religion debarred them from British universities, and to train priests. The families and progeny of these soldiers and scholars often kept contact with Ireland and in some cases England. Some set up trades, merchant houses and banks in parts of France and Spain, and to this day not a few of the most famous names in French wine and spirit production — Lynch and Hennessy, for example — are Irish. It has been estimated that in the 17th and 18th centuries nearly half a million Irish — about a quarter of the island's entire population in 1800 — were uprooted and settled on the continent.

As the world opened up in the 18th century, Irish emigrants found new ground to settle on. North America took a steady stream, especially of Ulster Presbyterians. Four of them signed the Declaration of Independence. A native of county Wexford, John Barry, earned the name of Father of the American Navy, and other Irishmen made their mark in every walk of public life, not least the amassing of millions through mining, road-building and railways. Numbers more went to Australia, sometimes in the chains of convict ships, sometimes as free fortune-seekers. New Zealand accepted many more. In India, where the laws restraining Catholics and other dissenters were less draconian, educated Irishmen were able to take jobs in the civil service which would have been denied them at home. Throughout the years of British rule, professional Irishmen made an extraordinary contribution to the administration of India and other colonies, while poorer settlers sowed the seeds of resentment and hatred of England which has not yet altogether abated.

Lola Montez, the beauty who captivated the king of Bavaria and provoked the revolution of 1848, was Irish. So was Count James Rice, who prepared a plan of the rescuing of Marie Antoinette. And General MacMahon, Duke of Magenta, who became President of France in 1873. And Bernardo O'Higgins, who became virtual dictator of newly independent Chile in 1817. And George Thompson who became ruler of the Indian state of Hariana. Berlioz's wife Harriet Smithson was Irish, as was Penelope Holroyd Smyth who became Princess of Capua. The exiled families of Nugent, Dillon and Teaffe ranked high among the aristocracy of the Austrian Empire. Napolcon's niece married an Irishman. So did the daughter of the philosopher Condorcet.

In terms of simple quantity, though, the total tally of all of these and many more exotic associations signified little against the number of Irish who migrated to Britain and America in the wake of the great famine of the late 1840s, and indeed well into this century. A combination of factors — the doubling of the Irish population in forty years,

197. A Dubliner with a look of the eternal student sells a magazine and a selection of postcards. The subjects range from a pint of Guinness with the Irish word for 'Cheers!' — Slainte (pronounced slawn-cher) to studies of Joyce, Behan , O'Casey and Shaw.

198

198 and 199. *Music accompanies the feasting at Bunratty Castle near Shannon Airport. The castle, a fine medieval structure heavily restored, was once the home of the O'Brien Earls of Thomond. At a banquet in 1276, the chief O'Brien was arrested here, bound, tied behind a team of horses and dragged to death. Modern banquets are less dangerous, and the music is probably a lot better performed.*

200. *A centrepiece example of modern Water-ford glass kept in the reception hall of the Water-ford Crystal Factory. Visitors can see the glass be-ing made. The quality is high, though the finest Waterford glass came out of the old factory, which closed in 1861 and had been at its best a decade or two before and after 1800.*

200

201

201. *A handsome golden eagle with wings outstretched.*

202. *The massive Dublin town house of the Wingfield, Viscounts Powerscourt (whose eponymous country house in Wicklow is noted for one of Ireland's most impressively sited gardens) has recently been converted into a shopping centre. Prior to this, for a hundred years and more it had served the modest function of warehouse and depot to a wholesale clothing firm.*

203. *Graffitti in Northern Ireland reflect the deep animosity between sections of the population. Loyalist flags flank the ancient symbol of Ulster, the Red Hand, while the Irish Republican flag, green, white and orange, is crudely captioned below.*

204. The ancient name for both city and county was Derry. When the City of London set large numbers of colonists in the early 17th century, the prefix London was appended. Nationalists object, as do thousands with moderate views who find the old name good enough.

205. Inner Belfast and inner Derry and other towns have been much affected by two decades of violence. Troops and armoured cars are commonplace, and barriers keep traffic out of vulnerable areas. The gutsy Northern Ireland population keeps even more cheerful than it is wont to be.

206. The original 19th-century Tudor revival building of the present Queen's University of Belfast. At first it was one constituent college of the university, the others being the Queen's Colleges of Galway and Cork. It was established as a full university in 1908, while the others joined with Dublin to make the National University of Ireland.

207. *The stately dining-room of Bantry House is surveyed by George III and his queen in copies of the Allen Ramsay paintings at the end. The room is composed of two different levels, the lower eighteenth century and the higher, separated by marble Ionic columns, belonging to the nineteenth century additions.*

208. *Bantry House, county Cork, built in 1765 for Richard White, who became first Earl of Bantry. The house overlooks Bantry Bay, one of whose islands, Whiddy, serves as an oil storage depot, tactfully camouflaged. The house was the first in Ireland to open to the public on a regular basis.*

209. *A mangnificient tapestry decorates the wall,
and a carpet of sumptuous design the floor.*

210. *Antother view of Bantry House, with the
owner, Mr Egerton Shelswell-White, whose un-
remitting efforts have maintained the condition of
the house through times when tourists were rare,
and continually improved the interiors. Most of
the finer contents were collected by the second
Earl of Bantry during travels on the continent in
the early 19th century.*

211. *Magnificent coloured tiles flank the simple chequerboard marble of the floor, in the entrance hall of Bantry House. The couloured titles are ancient Roman and were brought frim Pompeii.*

212. *Built in the last years of the 18th century, to the design of the prolific architect James Wyatt, Castle Coole in Fermanagh is often considered his finest work. No expense was spared, and the owner, the Earl of Belmore, died in 1802 deep in debt. The stone is from Portland on England's south coast (used among other buildings for St Paul's Cathedral).*

213. *A female statue sensitively sculpted to suggest the feel of skin and fine fabrics.*

214. *The 19th century brought a wave of Gothicising country houses. (At the same time innumerable families changed their names to give a medieval, often Norman ring). Where symmetry and simplicity had followed the dictates of the Age of Reason, the new Romantic fad brought riots of tower, turret, battlement and pointed arch.*

215

215. *The huge saloon of Emo Court, county Leix, begun for the Earl of Portarlington by James Gandon in 1790. This room, formerly the library, has a huge bow on the right, from whose windows can be seen the garden and park, all recently restored and replanted by the present owner.*

216. *Westport House, county Mayo, home of the Earls of Altamont. The handsome pedimented south front of the house is on the right. It was added to the existing building about 1780. The geese belong to the only breeding colony of greylags in the country.*

217. *The circular saloon at Castle Coole, county Fermanagh. The architect, James Wyatt, designed most of the fittings and furniture in the house, imposing a coherence over the whole.*

216

217

218. Laurence Parsons was granted a thousand acres of land at Birr, county Offaly, in 1620. In spite of subsequent shifts of regime and state religion in the 17th century, he and his family kept their heads, prospered, and continually increased the size of their castle which, seen here, mainly reflects an 1823 rebuilding.

219

219. *A line of portraits on the one side and pel-*
meted windows on the other deocrate the long
gallery, long enough for a walk on a rainy day,
as many old records testify.

220. *Bantry House, showing Bantry Bay in the background. In 1796 the patriot and soldier Wolfe Tone was blown here by storms in the ship the French had given him for a rebellion. The Bantry owner refused help or landing permission, and was rewarded with an earldom.*

222. *Kylemore Abbey on the shore of Kylemore Lake, an impressive extravaganza built in the late 19th century by a Liverpool millionaire. He also reclaimed much surrounding countryside from the bog, and planted trees and long vistas of rhododendron and fuchsia. Since the First World War the building has been a teaching convent of Benedictine nuns.*

221. 19th-century Blarney House, *next to Blarney Castle and seen here from the top of it. The estate usually belonged to the MacCarthy family. Both house and castle are open to the public, as are the extensive gardens.*

The potato blight destroyed the main means of sustenance of the Irish peasant, causing one million deaths from starvation and the same number of emigrants in a period of only five years.

an agricultural slump in the 1820s, and cheap passages to America in ships whose main income come from the transport of timber to Europe — had already raised numbers of transatlantic emigrants to new heights. During the 1830s something under 200,000 left for North America. But the famine outdid all these figures. The first impact was felt by Britain: Liverpool, with a population of 250,000, added 300,000 in the first few months of 1847, and had to feed and shelter them until the majority moved on to other parts of Britain or sailed to America. In less than five years a million left Ireland (and a million more died). Hundreds of thousands departed year by year from then on, aboard the new transatlantic steamers.

In America they stuck together, for shiploads of starving, sickly Catholics were not welcome among all sections of the population, least of all the Presbyterian Scots-Irish who made up the large part of previous immigrations. By 1870, Irish-born Irish outnumbered all other native-born groups with a total of 1,850,000. (Native-born Germans came next with 1,700,000.) They were primarily found in New York, Philadelphia, Boston, and the other towns of New York state, Massachusetts, Pennsylvania and, to a lesser degree, Ohio and Illinois. The undying memories of the famine gave them a greater unity than they might otherwise have had, at the heart of that unity being the resolve to rid Ireland of English rule, and to promote republicanism. This led them to finance and organise, right up to our own times, movements dedicated to the achievement of independence for all Ireland, by peaceful or violent means. It also pushed them into radical politics in their adopted land. For a considerable period some of them tainted democratic politics with the violence and corruption for which Tammany Hall became notorious. The rise of John F. Kennedy, Irish and Catholic, to the pinnacle of American power gave the Irish (in spite of the fact that the Kennedys maintained some of the worst as well as the best Democrat principles) a respectable status they had never fully enjoyed before.

Nobody in America has since neglected the Irish vote, for they wield huge electoral power. Americans of Irish descent outnumber the Irish of Ireland by four to one. No president, it seems, would tolerate staff who failed to find an Irishman in his ancestry, and a white-washed Irish cottage wherein his collateral family might still be found living modest, honest lives. Irish names abound in Senate and Congress, and in state and city governments. It is true that these American Irish are spread among all states, all professions and all income groups, and thoroughly integrated in the American way of life. But their strong attachment to Ireland remains. They visit their ancestral land in huge numbers, and support all manner of Irish causes, from arms-purchase to architecture.

With Britain things are rather different and rather difficult. There are about 750,000 Irish-born in the country. The number of those of Irish descent is beyond all calculation, the history of the two countries is so entwined. There is free passage between the countries, no restriction on employment, even a vote in the host country's elections. Yet the relationship is not entirely happy, nor would it be even if the question of the North were settled. Old attitudes die hard.

Ireland is still a mostly Catholic country isolated among northern Protestant ones. It may be the loneliness which makes her reach out readily to those she hopes to get on with: nowadays to the European community, to which she has rushed with open arms; to the United Nations, whose peacekeeping projects in the world's trouble-spots have often been manned by Irish troops; and to those parts of the world, spread across five continents, where she sends her monks and nuns and other personnel of her religious missions, just as she once sent her saints and scholars, all over the known world, to keep at bay the menace of barbarism.

Emigrants receive
a blessing before
setting off for the
New World,
with its promise
of a better life.

Important Dates in Irish History

432 St Patrick's arrival in Ireland to convert the pagan natives.

563 St Columba's mission to western Scotland and Iona.

590 St Columbanus' mission to the continent, ending at Bobbio near Milan.

664 Synod of Whitby. Irish monks lose arguments over Easter date and style of tonsure.

795 Norsemen begin to raid Ireland.

1014 High King Brian Boru defeats the Danes at Clontarf but is himself killed.

1166 Dermot MacMurrough leaves Ireland in search of allies.

1169 Welsh Normans land in Ireland.

1170 Strongbow follows other Normans to Ireland.

1171 Henry II comes to Ireland.

1172 Ireland granted to Henry II by Pope.

1315—1318 Ulster offers Edward Bruce the Irish crown. He overruns much of north and east Ireland, is crowned; then killed at Battle of Dundalk.

1366 Statutes of Kilkenny: attempt to bar integration of Anglo-Normans and native Irish.

1394 and 1399 Richard II's two visits to Ireland.

1477—1513 Garrett FitzGerald, Great Earl of Kildare, rules Ireland.

1487 The pretender Lambert Simnel crowned king in Dublin.

1494—1495 Poynings' Parliament. Poynings' Law makes acts of Irish parliaments dependent on approval of English parliament.

1534 Silken Thomas, tenth Earl of Kildare, revolts against English on the false information that his father has been executed in the Tower of London.

1535 Silken Thomas captured after siege of Maynooth.

1537 Silken Thomas and his five uncles executed in London.

1539 Commencement of the dissolution of the monasteries.

1541 Henry VIII becomes King instead of Lord of Ireland, and inaugurates Tudor policy of "surrender and regrant", intended to attract loyalty of Irish chieftains.

1549—1557 Plantations of Leix, renamed Queen's County, and Offaly, renamed King's County.

Irish warriors (drawing by Albrecht Durer).

1553—1558 Reign of Mary Tudor: temporary reversion to Roman Catholicism.

1567 Shane O'Neil killed at Cushendun, by the McDonnells, after vigorous campaigns to assert and exted his power against Queen Elizabeth's will.

1569 Irish Parliament resolves on the "reduction" of Ireland.

1569—1573 First Desmond Rebellion, caused by territorial and religious grievances.

1579—1583 Second Desmond Rebellion, ending with the death of the 15th Earl.

1586 Confiscation of more than half a million acres of last Earl of Desmond's territory in Munster; divided among English settlers, including Walter Raleigh.

1592 Foundation of Trinity College, Dublin.

1598 Victory of O'Neill and O'Donnell at the Yellow Ford.

1601 Defeat of O'Neill and O'Donnell at Kinsale.

1607 O'Neill and O'Donnell leave Ireland: "Flight of the Earls".

1608 Plantation of Ulster begins.

1632 Strafford becomes lord deputy.

1641 Ulster rebellion begins. Strafford executed in London.

1642 Owen Roe O'Neill arrives in Ulster. Formation of the Confederation of Kilkenny.

1646 Battle of Benburb: O'Neill victorious over Munro.

1649 Arrival in Ireland of Cromwell. Massacre at Drogheda followed by massacre at Wexford.

1652 Cromwell's Act of Settlement dispossesses many Catholic Irish.

1660 Charles II's restoration followed by considerable resettlement of land. Navigation and later acts discriminate against Ireland.

1685 James II succeeds his brother and reintroduces Catholicism.

1689 Siege of Derry by James's army. Relieved by William's navy.

1690 William III defeats James II at Battle of the Boyne. James flees to France.

1691 Siege of Limerick followed by Treaty of Limerick which brings war to end.

1695 First of the penal laws restricting the freedom of Catholics.

1699 English parliament restricts export of Irish woollen goods.

1719 Declaratory Act gives English parliament right to legislate for Ireland.

1724 Swift's *Drapier's Letters* published.

1729 Swift's *Modest Proposal* published.

1775 Henry Grattan leader of "Patriot Party".

1778 Irish Volunteers formed. Gardiner's Catholic Relief act begins the dismantling of the penal laws.

1782 Irish Volunteer convention at Dungannon, followed by Britain's grant of parliamentary independence.

1789 Start of the French Revolution.

1791 Formation of the Belfast and Dublin Societies of United Irishmen.

1796 Wolfe Tone in France. Attempted invasion of Ireland marred by storms in Bantry Bay.

1798 Arrest of Lord Edward FitzGerald and others of Leinster directory of United Irishmen. New French expedition with Tone on board defeated in Lough Swilly. Tone's suicide in captivity.

1800 Act of Union annuls separate Irish parliament.

1803 Robert Emmet's rebellion, capture and execution.

1808 Emergence of Daniel O'Connell in campaign to win Catholic emancipation.

1823 Foundation of Catholic Association.

1826 Pro-Catholic candidate Henry Villiers-Stuart wins Waterford election.

1828 O'Connell wins Clare election.

1829 Catholic Emancipation Act passed.

1843 O'Connell's monster meetings demand repeal of the Union.

1845 Potato blight reported.

1846 Repeal of the Corn Laws. Complete failure of the potato crop; harvest in following years is very poor.

1848 Young Ireland rising in Munster.

1858 Foundation of the Fenian movement.

1867 Fenian Risings in England and Ireland.

1869 Disestablishment of the Church of Ireland.

1870 Gladstone's first Land Act.

1877 Parnell becomes leader of Irish party at Westminster.

1879 Irish National Land League founded by Michael Davitt in Dublin.

1879—1882 The Land War, including the "Boycott" campaign.

1882 Assassination of new Chief Secretary Cavendish in Phoenix Park.

1886 Gladstone introduces first Home Rule Bill in House of Commons.

1890 O'Shea divorce case brings deposition of Parnell from leadership.

1891 Death of Parnell.

1893 Douglas Hyde founds Gaelic League. Gladstone's second Home Rule Bill defeated in House of Lords.

1902 Yeats founds National Theatre Society.

1905 Arthur Griffith founds Sinn Fein party.

1912 Third Home Rule Bill passed by House of Commons.

1913 Home Rule Bill defeated by House of Lords. Ulster Volunteer Force established. In Dublin, Irish Citizen Army and Irish Volunteers founded.

1914 Home Rule Bill passed, but its operation suspended for duration of war.

1916 Easter Rebellion, and proclamation of Irish Republic.

1919 Foundation of Dail Eireann, with De Valera as president. Anglo-Irish war begins.

1921 Northern Ireland parliament opens.

1922 Ratification of treaty between Britain and Irish Free State. Civil war in Ireland.

1927 De Valera's Fianna Fail party enters Dail.

1931 Statute of Westminster transforms British Empire into Commonwealth.

1932 Fianna Fail returned to power. De Valera prime minister till 1948. Economic war with Britain till 1938.

1936 External Relations Act makes Ireland a republic in all but a few technical respects.

1937 New Irish constitution confirms Ireland as a sovereign state, with the Catholic Church holding a special position.

1939—1945 Ireland remains neutral during Second World War, Belfast "blitzed" in 1941.

1949 Ireland finally an independent republic in all respects.

1955 Ireland a member of the United Nations.

1959 De Valera becomes president of Ireland.

1961 Application for membership of EEC turned down.

1965 Unprecedented meetings between prime ministers of Republic and North.

1968 Clash between police and Derry civil rights marchers heralds decades of terrorism.

1971 Ian Paisley's Democratic Unionist party founded.

1972 Ireland joins EEC.

Copy of the Proclamation of the Republic, read by Patrick Pearse from the steps of the GPO building, Dublin, during the Easter Rising of 1916.

THE PROCLAMATION OF
POBLACHT NA H EIREANN.
THE PROVISIONAL GOVERNMENT
OF THE
IRISH REPUBLIC
TO THE PEOPLE OF IRELAND.

IRISHMEN AND IRISHWOMEN: In the name of God and of the dead generations from which she receives her old tradition of nationhood, Ireland, through us, summons her children to her flag and strikes for her freedom.

Having organised and trained her manhood through her secret revolutionary organisation, the Irish Republican Brotherhood, and through her open military organisations, the Irish Volunteers and the Irish Citizen Army, having patiently perfected her discipline, having resolutely waited for the right moment to reveal itself, she now seizes that moment, and, supported by her exiled children in America and by gallant allies in Europe, but relying in the first on her own strength, she strikes in full confidence of victory.

We declare the right of the people of Ireland to the ownership of Ireland, and to the unfettered control of Irish destinies, to be sovereign and indefeasible. The long usurpation of that right by a foreign people and government has not extinguished the right, nor can it ever be extinguished except by the destruction of the Irish people. In every generation the Irish people have asserted their right to national freedom and sovereignty; six times during the past three hundred years they have asserted it in arms. Standing on that fundamental right and again asserting it in arms in the face of the world, we hereby proclaim the Irish Republic as a Sovereign Independent State, and we pledge our lives and the lives of our comrades-in-arms to the cause of its freedom, of its welfare, and of its exaltation among the nations.

The Irish Republic is entitled to, and hereby claims, the allegiance of every Irishman and Irishwoman. The Republic guarantees religious and civil liberty, equal rights and equal opportunities to all its citizens, and declares its resolve to pursue the happiness and prosperity of the whole nation and of all its parts, cherishing all the children of the nation equally, and oblivious of the differences carefully fostered by an alien government, which have divided a minority from the majority in the past.

Until our arms have brought the opportune moment for the establishment of a permanent National Government, representative of the whole people of Ireland and elected by the suffrages of all her men and women, the Provisional Government, hereby constituted, will administer the civil and military affairs of the Republic in trust for the people.

We place the cause of the Irish Republic under the protection of the Most High God, Whose blessing we invoke upon our arms, and we pray that no one who serves that cause will dishonour it by cowardice, inhumanity, or rapine. In this supreme hour the Irish nation must, by its valour and discipline and by the readiness of its children to sacrifice themselves for the common good, prove itself worthy of the august destiny to which it is called.

Signed on Behalf of the Provisional Government,

THOMAS J. CLARKE,

SEAN Mac DIARMADA,   THOMAS MacDONAGH,
P. H. PEARSE,   EAMONN CEANNT,
JAMES CONNOLLY.   JOSEPH PLUNKETT